ENDORSEMENTS

W hen Ken came to work for me, I was impressed but skeptical. He was a fairly senior officer with only a few years' experience in the technical aspects of running a hospital. I wasn't sure how best to place him in our organization. He quickly allayed my fears because of his leadership qualities. I now realize his success was due to the Model he brought from his flying days. Give it a shot, you'll be glad you did. It will help you get your organization off the ground and to your desired destination."

—Allen Middleton,

Former Deputy Assistant Secretary of Defense (Health Budgets & Financial Policy); Former Deputy Director, Defense Health Agency; 15th chief of the Air Force Medical Service Corps.

"I think the Model Ken crafted by melding his flying and business experience has the potential to revolutionize leader development. My connection with Ken is multi-faceted. As Dean of the Smeal College of Business at Penn State, Ken served as an Instructor for both our soft skill (i.e., leadership) and hard skill (i.e., accounting) courses. As President of our local medical center's governance board,

I've also had the pleasure to observe Ken, a board member. These connections have allowed me to watch Ken offer insightful solutions as both teacher and board member. As a friend, I believe Ken is a man of integrity who truly desires to help people unlock, engage, and optimize their potential. I'm excited to see the positive impact 'On Course' has in both the business and academic world."

—Dr. James B. Thomas,
Elliott Professor of Risk and Management,
Immediate past Dean, Smeal College of Business, PSU

"As a Millennial workplace expert, I work to ensure people in organizations communicate effectively. I believe the Successful Ventures in Human Dynamics Model has significant potential to bridge gaps between people of various generations. Give it a try—I think you will be happy with your results."

—Lindsey Pollak,
New York Times Bestselling Author of "Becoming the Boss:
New Rules for the Next Generation of Leaders"

"I've known and worked with Ken Pasch as a professional colleague for many years, and I'm proud to say he and KiVisions have done a simply masterful job of taking the incredibly complex topic of leadership and breaking it down into simple, people-focused techniques that really work. Further, their Successful Ventures in Human Dynamics model is easily understood. Leaders at all levels can use this model to improve their operations while simultaneously allowing the people working with them, both internally and externally, to unlock, engage, and optimize their potential and lead a much more fulfilling life, both personally and professionally."

—Steve Brown,
FACHE, Healthcare CEO (retired)

"With On Course, author Ken Pasch makes an important contribution to the literature on leadership. He challenges you the reader to ask tough questions about your own leadership approach, then offers a structured model that will help you to be the best leader you can be. One of the things that makes this book unique is the way Ken has woven his experiences as a military aviator into his leadership model. Every leader, regardless of their experience level or their field of endeavor, can benefit from the wisdom and the strategies that Ken shares in this book."

—Joe Tye,
CEO and Head Coach, Values Coach Inc. and author of
"All Hands on Deck: 8 Essential Lessons for Building a Culture"

"I had the good fortune to watch a portion of the material in On Course, in action! I am a trusted adviser for an entrepreneur that needed to ensure his "plane" was pointed in the right direction. During a retreat for this entrepreneur that Ken facilitated a "magical" transformation occurred. Our entrepreneur found his path. Plus, he now had a complement of tools to stay on that path. I highly recommend you not only read but adopt the principles taught in this book!"

—Joe Harteis,
President of Harteis Enterprises

"While serving with Ken in the Air Force Medical Service, it became obvious he was a forward thinking individual who fully understood the concept of "we." It is safe to say a totalitarian management style would not have fared well in our organization. As Chief Master Sergeants (Product Line Managers in civilian health care organizations), one of our primary concerns was ensuring the welfare of our airmen (employee associates), which, in turn, ensured our mission to provide optimal care for our patients was successful. Ken's leadership style allowed us to openly share our concerns and do so with the understanding he would listen and apply corrective actions, based on our recommendations, to resolve problems. The bottom line is he was already applying the concepts of the Successful Ventures in

Human Dynamics Model. His asking for our input and including our feedback in his resolution tactics served to increase Lift throughout the organization. His application of our recommendations provided the Thrust we needed to ensure our medical center met or exceeded the needs of our patients. Most importantly, the ownership afforded to our staff, who worked so diligently ensuring our patients were well cared for, allowed them to be more fulfilled. Our recommendation: "Use the Model and become a Great Leader."

—Chief Master Sergeants (Retired),
United States Air Force, Ron Beckett & Jack Perry

"Becoming a great leader can be learned and Ken Pasch has proven it in his new book, "On Course". This book has shown me that leadership is a skill and like any other skill, must be developed and practiced. Ken shows you how to become aware of what needs done then take action to do it."

—Lynn Brown,
Founder & CEO, Command Connections Speakers Bureau

"Ken and I designed and piloted a graduate level course at Penn State. Together, we produced an awesome learning experience for our students. The framework for leadership outlined in his book helps me better understand the basis of his ideas that we used for that course. As a result, I have no doubt "On Course" will help you better lead your team."

—Daniel J. Geltrude, CPA

"I have stayed connected with Ken since my days as a student at Penn State because I have appreciated his mentorship. I was excited to have my leadership at Janssen Pharmaceuticals partner with Ken to train and develop our people. His Successful Ventures in Human Dynamics model helps me realize the need to balance those factors that impact the outcome of the decisions I make. The model *also provides a great frame of reference that I can "keep in my head" whenever I am faced with an issue I must resolve. Plus, knowing that KiVisions has the material and support structure I need as I continue on my leadership journey brings me great comfort…I no longer have to walk this path alone."*

—Catherine Milano,

Health Care Compliance Officer, Johnson & Johnson

"After years of struggling with the direction of my own company that provides personal and professional growth and development training, I asked Ken to fa-cilitate a retreat with my Advisory Council. Using materials from his book, On Course, worked amazingly well. I "changed course" and have a clear vision and focus like we have never experienced. I can't thank Ken enough. We are on track to significantly exceed many of our existing benchmarks and future goals. Follow his plan and you will achieve similar success."

—Rick Capozzi,

Founder/President, SurvivalMindset

"As a student, I have had multiple opportunities to work and engage with Ken. He has shaped the minds and identities of many students. Instead of simply looking at what answers students produce, he is a professor that encourages stu-dents to find value in searching for answers. My own perceptions have much greater depth thanks to his guidance. Before reading "On Course", I did not feel comfortable, or even qualified, to assume leadership roles. It was an ethereal, nearly-unattainable trait that was reserved only for those "reckoned" as leaders. This book helped me break down the arbitrary definitions, and replace them with a much more practical interpretation of the role. "On Course" gave me the courage to recognize the quality of leadership as achievable by anyone."

—Grace Hill,

Finance Student, Penn State University

ON
become a great
leader and soar
COURSE

KEN PASCH

Foreword by Brig. General (ret) Peter Bellisario

NEW YORK

NASHVILLE • MELBOURNE • VANCOUVER

ON COURSE

Published in New York, New York, by Morgan James Publishing. Morgan James and The Entrepreneurial Publisher are trademarks of Morgan James, LLC.
www.MorganJamesPublishing.com

The Morgan James Speakers Group can bring authors to your live event. For more information or to book an event visit The Morgan James Speakers Group at
www.TheMorganJamesSpeakersGroup.com.

The John Maxwell Company has extended permission to include the passages in this book that come from "The Maxwell Plan".

www.KiVisions.com
KiVisions, Inc. donates approximately 10% of all income to the KiVisions Fund. The Fund's purpose is to increase the potential for people to live in greater peace, freedom, and prosperity.

ISBN 978-1-68350-513-6 paperback
ISBN 978-1-68350-514-3 eBook
Library of Congress Control Number: 2017905001

Cover & Interior Design by:
Megan Whitney
Creative Ninja Designs
megan@creativeninjadesigns.com

In an effort to support local communities, raise awareness and funds, Morgan James Publishing donates a percentage of all book sales for the life of each book to Habitat for Humanity Peninsula and Greater Williamsburg.

Get involved today! Visit
www.MorganJamesBuilds.com

To Mom, Dad, Gramma, and Grampa: I hope the part I play

in making the world a better place conveys my gratitude

to you. I love you all very much!

CONTENTS

CONTENTS

FOREWORD

I t is with pleasure that I introduce you to a treatise written by Ken Pasch.

Ken and I served together on active duty in the United States Air Force. From our first meeting in San Antonio, Texas, I was immediately impressed with Ken's style. I saw him transition from a successful flying career as an Air Force B52 crewmember into the USAF Medical Service Corp (MSC). This move was courageous at the time, but one he desired to undertake to broaden the vector of his air force career. To say that his leadership role then was one of inexperience is true, but what has since transpired within Ken and the organizations he has led is truly remarkable.

Great leaders possess the ability and desire to mentor their replacements. I have fond memories of a senior general officer "passing the baton" to me. From then on, I felt a significant responsibility to mentor young officers. Ken was one of those officers in whom I saw great potential, and I never questioned my "passing the baton" to him. By following his KiVisions leadership model, he is "passing the baton" to you through this book.

Even though I was his boss, we were stationed hundreds of miles apart. I trusted Ken to be my eyes, ears, and often my voice as he contended with officers more senior than him. Coming from all three services, they were convinced their way was the only way. As the junior officer in this group, Ken held the line. It took great integrity and confidence for him to do this.

My colleagues and I saw unlimited potential in Ken. We mentored him, stepped back, and gave him added responsibility and command. The departmental improvements under his watch and his amazing transformation into a respected and trusted leader became evident.

After a distinguished 20 years of service in the U.S. Air Force, Ken has forged a successful career in the private sector. He revamped an antiquated core business course at Pennsylvania State University and received numerous awards and accolades from students, administrators, and business leaders.

Ken's diversified successes in the fields of military, academia, and private business give him the credentials to serve you well in your desire to become a great leader who will make a difference. Above all, Ken's adherence to his love of family, faith, and country as well as his respect for his fellow man are overriding principles that form the basis of this book.

Looking back, I can see how Ken applied his flying experience to the model you'll learn about in this book, which employs the relationship between getting both an aircraft and an organization off the ground successfully.

You'll find this book is about both the "art" and the "doing." Ken's model not only represents his growth as a leader but will assist you as you apply this leadership model in your own leadership journey. Your results will be remarkable!

Have you found your purpose? Ken has found his: Helping Good People Become Great Leaders. And he shares it with you here.

Best wishes as you journey toward success.

—Brigadier General (Retired) Peter Bellisario

PREFACE

Helping the world become a better place starts with a willingness to explore possibilities. I've been fortunate to learn from thousands, even my dogs, who have taught me unconditional love. Although my thoughts in this book are my own, they've been tempered by all my "teachers".

Learning allows each of us to study one another's ideas without necessarily buying into everything offered. In that vein, I encourage you to respectfully challenge my assumptions or rationale. I love good, honest debate. Let's learn from each other.

To provide viable input into this quest that will help the world become a better place, I have invested years researching, exploring, and pondering how to bring this vision to fruition. I uncovered resources that can help more people live in relative peace, freedom, and prosperity—in fact, they're plentiful. The "missing" ingredient is the proper mindset: Instead of touting an "I Win" mentality, I challenged myself to adopt a "We Win" mindset. As you read this book, I challenge you to do the same. You will likely find it helps in many aspects of your life.

But on a larger scale, how can our society achieve a better to-morrow? It requires all of us who are unsatisfied with current conditions to embrace the desire and develop the capability to become Great Leaders. Our efforts can be magnified if we follow a process proven to achieve stunning results. To this end, I spent *twenty* years developing and testing the three components of the KiVisions Leader Development Process: a model leaders can employ, a system that makes employing that model as simple as possible, and the challenge to keep leaders motivated along their journey. (Caution: There's nothing simple about leading people.)

How I Was Drawn to My Great Leaders Vision

The key incident that led me to develop this Leader Development Process happened in 1972, a horrible year for me. I was one of the last people in our country to be drafted into the U.S. Army. With young Americans dying in the jungles during the Vietnam War, I feared my life would be over. But I got lucky. I received a reprieve from active duty and was allowed to return to college under the ROTC Program (Reserve Officers Training Corps). As soon as I was able, I exchanged my Army "greens" for Air Force "blues." This allowed me to do something I never would have had the opportunity to do otherwise—fly! As this book explains, my flying experience provided the solution to the single greatest professional issue I ever faced: learning to lead.

How I came to value the potential in humans is a long story. Earlier in my life, school bored me. Why did I have to learn all that stuff? My lack of desire put me behind my peers. Because I didn't work hard, some people thought I was stupid, and they openly offered their opinions on the subject. At one time, I didn't even believe I knew how to think.

I only went to college because my dad made me. Getting through was a struggle the first couple of years and so was picking a major. At the time, I had no idea why I chose to study Health Policy Administration. About that time, I got drafted. The armed forces wasn't in my game plan, and I wasn't happy. But thankfully, I found the silver lining to that cloud in my life. And flying came easy to me.

As I look back, there was nothing "easy" about learning to fly. How is it possible that someone who was thought to be "stupid" was able to manage the difficult curriculum required of flyers? This helped me form the impression that things we *like* to do are *easier* to do. That's especially true when we have dedicated people showing us how.

Because I liked flying and had great teachers, I focused on it and—a major surprise to my parents—I won lots of awards. This sequence of events helped me understand that all humans have potential, real potential!

I only flew professionally for about six years, fulfilling my commitment to the Air Force. If I loved it so much, you may wonder, why did I quit doing it? Because flying in the military is not easy on families. A number of my friends went through painful divorces. At the time, it was heartbreaking to give up flying, but I know my wife and kids suffered for years due to the long hours I spent preparing, planning, flying, debriefing, being on hair-trigger alert status, and deploying to parts unknown.

Most people don't do well with the unknown. Here's an example of something that to me was an adventure but to my wife was a long nightmare. I got a 3:00 a.m. phone call with orders to report to the squadron by 6:00 a.m. and plan on being gone for at least thirty days.

That's it, and because of the classification of the mission, my next contact with my family happened when I showed up forty-five days later. Decades later, I'm *still* not allowed to tell my wife what that mission was all about.

Next Step: Hospital Administrator

Out of legitimate frustration, she said, "Either you stay flying *or* we stay married." I realized I had to grow up and get a "real" job. Yet I saw in those six years how incredibly important the military is to maintaining our civil society and I enjoyed being part of something good. So I looked for opportunities within the U.S. Air Force. My Health Policy Administration degree plus a Master's Degree in Business I earned while flying allowed me to compete for a position as a Medical Service Corps officer (a hospital administrator).

Becoming a Medical Service Corps officer led to two epiphanies: First, I had to kick it into high gear just to keep up with the incredible officers where I was stationed. Talented and hard-working, they were achieving astonishing results. Second, although flying came with serious responsibilities, I had only been leading myself. For the first time, I was put into a position of authority and was expected to lead others. Unfortunately, I only did okay as a supervisor, administrator, and manager but that wasn't good enough. I sucked at leading. For example, because I was "in charge," I assumed people would do things to the best of their ability because I dictated what I wanted. Oh, how wrong I was. This gave me plenty of motivation to find a solution.

I tried learning leadership skills from books, courses, and workshops, but nothing sunk in. After many sleepless nights, I had this epiphany: "Could it be that what it takes to get an organization off the ground is similar to what it takes to get an airplane off the ground?"

This idea for becoming a better leader evolved into a flying-related model, which you'll learn about in this book.

Helping Good People Become Great Leaders

Throughout my journey, I've continually transformed my company to ensure it achieves the singular purpose of *helping good people become Great Leaders*. My staff and I teach and mentor, coach and consult. By doing our jobs, this Process becomes a catalyst for achieving the vision of a better world. I'm betting my legacy on this outcome.

After developing, testing, and fine-tuning the Process, we can expand exponentially. We offer *all good people who want to become Great Leaders* the opportunity to learn and apply it. The result? You become an incredible influence in your world.

This book, *On Course*, leads the way.

INTRODUCTION

What are your daytime dreams—the ones that get you out of bed in the morning?

Accomplishing our dreams can leave us fulfilled and the world better than we found it. Many of us were lucky enough to be born in a country where this was possible. Unfortunately, I think our society has fallen off course. As a baby boomer, I'm afraid my kids and grandkids won't be able to achieve their dreams. Something needs to change, but it will take all of us who are unsatisfied with our current conditions to have an impact.

In the early history of the U.S., our founders had divine inspiration. Sure, they had their flaws and foibles, and some of their actions would be unacceptable in today's society. But they took on the grand mission of forming an ideal union. They wanted to create the first country in history to allow people—regardless of their place in society—to achieve their dreams.

These founders had no self-serving reason to accept this grand mission. In fact, they likely understood the damage to their reputations and fortunes that would result by fighting for freedom. They could have sat in their pubs, quaffed their ale, and whined about how bad things were. Thankfully, they had the fortitude to give you and me an incredible gift—the framework of an exceptional nation.

I thank them and all who have sacrificed to give us this gift, one we shouldn't squander. Their collective efforts eventually led to the American Dream of increased peace, freedom, and prosperity for millions of people around the world.

Do you believe, as I do, that this dream is a worthy cause to pursue?

What Can You Expect from *On Course?*

This book starts by helping you discover why the American society, collectively, has gotten Off Course. Next, you are given tips and tools to help you get your world On Course and stay there. As more people sign on to become Great Leaders, there's a greater likelihood our society will get back On Course.

And what's not in this book? A quick fix—because there ain't no such thing. If that's what you're looking for, it may be your frustration speaking. I get that. I've been there. It's like the pain I suffered when I identified my lack of leader skills that pushed me to find a solution. By implementing ideas in this book, you can be making progress, but it will take a long time to understand and fully use all that's necessary. Learning "how to" and then successfully leading people requires a lifelong effort to transform, break down myths, and play a role in helping society achieve greater peace, freedom, and prosperity.

It is within our reach.

After reading *On Course*, you will understand that this "soft skill" called leadership is not made up. Indeed, you'll learn how practical it can be while realizing the importance of becoming a Great Leader.

Specifically, you'll learn to:

✦ Unlock, Engage, and Optimize (UEO) your innate potential

✦ Become an ACE—live with an **A**bundance mentality, **C**oncentrate on priorities, and **E**arnestly pursue your purpose with passion

✦ Get ready to learn the definition of and steps toward becoming a True Leader, which leads to becoming a Great Leader. Our KiVisions Leader Development Process helps you achieve both.

✦ Understand that to serve as a Breakthrough Leader requires intensity, integrity, and commitment. It becomes the pinnacle of achievement in the leader world.

What Does It Take to Become an ACE?

Do you have what it takes to become an ACE? A True Leader? A Great Leader? A Breakthrough Leader?

Yes, you do—or you wouldn't search for ways to make things better. Let's work though the leadership issues you face. Society needs you to break through barriers and make the American Dream possible for all.

The primary outcome for Great Leaders is to *unlock, engage, and optimize* their potential while inspiring the same in those they lead.

Their greatest quest becomes developing new Great Leaders who can keep us On Course toward a better tomorrow.

It's a fact that humans are selfishly motivated to ensure their survival. It takes Great Leaders to help people understand the beauty and benefits of growing beyond their selfish nature to a point of selflessly sharing an Abundance Mentality. To make significant progress, it's necessary to *concentrate on priorities and earnestly pursue our purpose with passion!*

Becoming an ACE requires you to toss off the yoke of limitations you and others have placed around your neck. Realize the incredible potential inside you and others. Join me on this journey and *soar!*

chapter one
OFF COURSE

An audience participant of a keynote once challenged me to prove my postulation that our country, many organizations, and too many individuals are Off Course. I love challenges like this. They force me to examine my work for any "holes". To validate my position, I came up with 5 Key Questions to clarify if we're On or Off Course. They pertain to our society as a whole but have deep significance for everyone as well. See if you agree.

What Are the 5 Key Questions?

1. As a society, are we on the cusp of a major breakthrough to heal those factors that divide us?

2. Are we as safe and secure as possible from threats to our health and way of life?

3. Are we making decisions that keep us on a bright path to greater prosperity?

4. Are we willing to testify to the value of everything we produce and the services we provide?

5. Are we soaring (that is, living truly fulfilling lives)?

If we could answer yes to each of the 5 Key Questions, would that indicate we're on the right path? If not, are we Off Course?

> What do you think about these 5 Key Questions? Please email your thoughts to KiVisions@KiVisions.com with the subject "5 Key Questions."

Exploring answers to each of these questions involves considering both positive and negative aspects. To discern whether the ultimate answer is yes or no, you can use an approach called On Net: *Accurately compare the pluses and minuses, determine which aspects carry more weight or have higher relative importance, and factor the change in weighting in your final decision.* When deciding critical issues, be careful how you derive your On Net conclusions.

Let me add the following caveats to the 5 Key Questions:

✦ Let's not take shortcuts that dispose of high ethical and moral standards to reach solutions to these questions.

✦ Let's ensure safeguarding freedom is a priority, not an afterthought.

✦ Let's ensure our education systems prepare our youth to tackle life's challenges. In addition, we need to ensure viable retraining opportunities for adults. Education is one of my biggest concerns.

✦ Let's be proud of the work we do enough to ensure people know "I did that," just as the signers of the Declaration of Independence once did.

✦ Let's not be worried about the consequences of accepting responsibility for what we have/have not done.

On a personal level, the 5 Key Questions boil down to a fairly simple metric: Can you honestly say, "I am soaring, I am living a truly fulfilling life"? On a societal or national scale, *how many* people can honestly say this?

My friend can, as this case study explains.

A Case for Inspired Work

A friend of mine is a local business man with multiple interests, one of which is a dairy farm. He was asked to entertain a contingent of researchers from a country that had a centrally planned economy at the time of their visit. (This country no longer exists in the form it did when they visited.) My friend showed them his entire venture. The researchers were impressed with the magnitude of the operation and wondered how many people worked on the farm. When my friend responded "just me," they were speechless. They openly doubted the veracity of his claim because their centrally planned economy didn't provide incentive for individuals to work hard and be innovative. In that situation, success was limited.

The opportunity to UEO human potential is necessary at multiple levels: nationally, organizationally, and individually. In my friend's case, he is fortunate to live in a country that allows him the opportunity to UEO his potential. But his success is also due to his "drive" to make the most of his talents.

We must ensure we maintain that opportunity to achieve fulfillment for all citizens. We must provide opportunities in our organizations and promote individuals as role models to help others realize the benefits of soaring. Getting to "yes" with the 5 Key Questions will help.

I contend that unless we make a drastic course correction, the American Dream might become another relic of history—or worse yet, the American Nightmare. If either of these scenarios happens, it would be a shame because millions would suffer, both here and around the world.

The Importance of Leaders Getting Back On Course

As our population ages, competition for talented employees will become the primary issue for business leaders. Many believe young people are naturally proficient with technology, but that's not true. Also, because the population is aging so quickly, issues we haven't dealt with before will emerge due to the numbers of baby boomers and their longevity.

Human capital is the catalyst that releases the value in all other resources. Taking care of people needs to be job #1 for all those who aspire to be True Leaders.

Without a properly chosen, informed, developed, trained, equipped, measured, rewarded, and inspired staff, all other capital formations—both tangible and intangible—will fail to generate optimum value. Plus, most businesses today rely on talent that's not easily replaceable or interchangeable because skill sets are becoming so specialized. Organizations must work to ensure they attract the best and the brightest.

Some people are attracted by material wealth. I, for one, am more interested in those who desire to fully unlock, engage, and optimize their potential. Of course that doesn't mean I expect people to work for free; those who perform well should be rewarded handsomely. Part of that reward should be the opportunity to give their life real meaning by engaging in that which "drives" them, their passion.

Leadership Versus Management

Organizations need to ask the critical question of whether they are leading or managing people. The words *lead* and *manage* are often used interchangeably, people may not understand the distinction. But only one of these is possible.

Here's an example. Pick up a pencil and do your best to determine the resources and processes that went into producing that pencil. If you used those same resources and processes, could you duplicate that pencil? Obviously, the answer is yes.

Now let's consider the person responsible for gathering, refining, or manipulating the resources needed to produce that pencil. Can you guarantee that person will bring those resources to the organization on any given day? The obvious answer is no.

So why not mechanize everything and get humans out of the equation? *Because humans bring much more to the equation than resources.* They bring creativity, innovation, ideas, and more. They can subjectively discern the need to improve a process or, better yet, determine how to creatively replace a process. People can collaboratively decide what that improvement or replacement should look like. The rationale for keeping humans involved is quite long.

The best idea is to *lead people and manage resources/tasks.* The resources people bring to the organization—their time, talent, education, certifications, and so on—can be managed. *Managing* implies mostly objective measurements. (For example, was the most recent project completed on time and within budgetary constraints?) *Leading*, on the other hand, requires mostly subjective measurements. I have yet to find anyone who was born with a Monroney sticker (as seen on new cars) that indicates what's inside.

Great Leaders develop the ability to help those they work with understand they have more potential than they realize and then apply that potential.

Dr. Abraham Maslow documented what he called the Hierarchy of Needs.[1] They are:

+ Self-actualization
+ Esteem
+ Love/belonging
+ Safety
+ Physiological

Let me offer my explanation to his theory. As you ascend the pyramid he portrayed, I believe the urgency expressed by "*need* to achieve ever higher levels" is diminished. We can all relate to the "need" to meet the physiological aspects he describes on the first level of his pyramid. Too few people naturally believe in a "need" to "self-actualize"—the highest level on his pyramid.

There is a large segment of people who "desire" to achieve self-actualization but, without getting help, they're not likely to do what it takes to reach this level. The reason: a number of factors, including fear that overwhelms desire. It takes a Great Leader to help group members overcome those factors. As sentient beings, most people need help to achieve fulfillment.

With those who have best talent, leading is even more necessary because these people aren't easily replaced. A high priority for every executive is properly employing human capital. The business strategy itself may be at risk if people aren't led effectively.

Past and Present

As members of American society, were we On Course in our past? At the founding of our country? Since then?

It used to be a given that the current generation of adults would leave the world a better place for their kids and grandkids. Do you believe that's true today? I'm not convinced it is, but I do believe we can get back On Course, as this book explains.

The history of our country hasn't been smooth. Our forebears accepted horrendous situations as "normal." We've had to make serious course corrections, such as abolishing slavery and ensuring African Americans and women have the right to vote. Fortunately, the Founding Fathers gave us a course correction process for addressing these "warts"—the U.S. Constitution. Check out the following Constitutional Amendments as evidence of the process we use to address our "warts":

- ✦ Amendment 13: Abolition of Slavery
- ✦ Amendment 14: Right to be free from discrimination; to have due process of law; to have equal protection of the law
- ✦ Amendment 15: African-Americans' Right to Vote
- ✦ Amendment 19: Women's Right to Vote

Our country can serve as a role model to ensure dehumanizing practices are eliminated around the world. In many places, slavery is still acceptable and women's right to vote is still not honored.

Complexity and Sacrifice

Has the entire world become too complex? In addition to the Civil War and the suffrage movement, we've led other nations in dealing with highly complex issues. Like other countries, we've contended with the Great Depression, World Wars I and II, the Korean War, the Vietnam War, and the Cold War. We've also dealt with a number of economic and other crises that questioned our faith in humans' ability to do the right things. In attempts to resolve them, they each brought further complexity.

Currently, certain ongoing issues could shake the fabric of our nation and our world. Will we have the intestinal fortitude to do what it takes to get us back On Course?

Before embarking on this journey to be a Great Leader, you have to decide: As the band Linkin Park asks, *Are you on the side of "Burn It Down," or do you believe there's something worth saving?* Many have paid the ultimate sacrifice. What did they believe in so deeply that made them feel their sacrifices were worth it? And why do people continue to make these sacrifices?

Sacrifices for Freedom

When you consider the gifts of living in society, you may realize certain things are worth safeguarding going forward. Here are a few examples of sacrifices for freedom from U.S. history:

+ On June 17, 1775, a bunch of farmers and merchants took on the world's most powerful army of its time at Bunker Hill.

+ During the U.S. Civil War, over three days in July 1863 at a small town in southern Pennsylvania (just south of where I live), more than 50,000 casualties were suffered.

+ In October 1918 during World War I, men from the U.S. 77th Division kept up the fight against a larger German force encircling them in the Argonne Forest in France. Sketchy records set the total number of men who began the engagement between 550 and 680. Subsequently, this group was given the historic moniker of The Lost Battalion. Only 194 men walked out of this fight; the rest were killed, captured, missing, or too exhausted to leave the battlefield on their own.

> ## Survivor of Argonne
>
> My grandfather on my mother's side, Thomas Francis Donato, was one of the survivors in The Lost Battalion and earned a Purple Heart from that battle. He and I were very close. Through the years, he graciously answered his grandson's questions and told me much of what went on in that forest.
>
> The key lesson he taught me (although I didn't "get it" as a kid) was the importance of leadership. Even after suffering heartbreaking casualties that included many of his friends, my grandfather revered Major Charles Whittlesey, who was in charge of the battalion. The men knew Whittlesey was doing everything he could to get them out alive and with honor.

+ During World War II, the U.S. lost more people to combat than in any war previously or since.

+ U.S. Armed Forces got involved in Korea a few years after World War II.

+ U.S. Armed Forces served in Vietnam from 1959 to 1973.

+ U.S. Armed Forces served in Iraq (Phase 1) in the early 1990s

+ U.S. Armed Forces' involvement in Afghanistan began in October 2001 (in response to 9/11)

+ U.S. Armed Forces' involvement in Iraq again, beginning in March 2003 (Phase 2).

✦ U.S. troops today could be engaged in a major offensive against ISIS, Iraq Phase 3, Syria, Libya, and the list could go on.

The Korean War

I highly recommend the book *Marine! The Life of Chesty Puller* by Burke Davis. General Puller is *the* most decorated U.S. marine. This book gives you a glimpse of what U.S. armed forces went through. Why would they do this?

In studying American history related to the brave young men and women who fought, I was astonished to learn they knew they were putting themselves in harm's way but did it anyway. Why? What did they believe in so deeply that it made them believe their sacrifices were worthwhile? Well, either they were bloodthirsty killers with no other options in life or they believed the cause was worth fighting and possibly dying for.

I served in the U.S. Air Force for more than twenty years. In all that time, out of the thousands of people I met and worked with, I can honestly say I met only one—that's right, one—who joined up for the sole purpose of killing. And he didn't last long in our culture. Plus, the vast majority of those I served with had options. Their service came from a deep belief in something they felt was important—not their only means to put food on the table.

Because many people did put themselves in harm's way for freedom and country, including my family, I must honor their sacrifice by living my dream. And I want to keep the dream alive for others who will one day walk in my footsteps.

As you think about what this country offers and what you're grateful for, are you willing to take up this mantle and carry it to others? Are you willing to make your own sacrifices and learn to lead the change to get this country On Course?

chapter two
DISENGAGEMENT AND DISTRACTIONS

ncredible advancements in technology have changed the scope of work from mostly physical to mostly mental pursuits. Conditions for those in physical career fields have improved with tools and other enhancements. These advanced conditions have yielded a greater energy residual at the end of each work day and extended life spans so people can enjoy the fruits of their labor.

In addition to reducing physical abuse to our bodies compared with previous generations, much of the extended life span people benefit from is due to modern medical innovations. The net gain: *We've significantly reduced the physical effort and pain required to meet our basic needs.*

> ## "If Everything is So Amazing, Why's Nobody Happy?"
>
> That's a comment from comedian Louis C. K. (See his YouTube video at https://www.youtube.com/watch?v=q8LaT5Iiwo4)

It's not funny, though. Most of us can afford to fulfill our needs. But somehow our desires, as unrealistic as they might be, take precedence. Focusing on unfulfilled desires can create a downward spiral that causes many to never find happiness or fulfillment.

Two-Edged Sword

Contemporary life can be a two-edged sword in this way: Many people in the U.S. have achieved levels of wealth never before seen on a mass scale. But now that so many of us have "made it," can we stay in that place in equally large or greater numbers?

Let's face it. More people in America have gone from "rags to riches" than in any other country at any other point in history. It's easy to assume the system that created this wealth is sustainable, but many wonder about this. Yes, I believe we can continue to improve our way of life—*if* many good people commit to becoming Great Leaders.

The Void

Another problem: Most humans are not fully confident in their decisions and actions. As a result, they crave feedback. The physical pursuits of our ancestors provided immediate feedback. In those days, if you did the job; you saw how well it was done.

In our past, we could see the fields we plowed and the fruit we picked—tangible results. Later in human history, fewer people worked on farms, but most still worked in jobs with results they could see such as cars they helped build rolling off the assembly line. As time goes by, more and more of our efforts are spent on less and less tangible results. It's become increasingly difficult for our bosses to help us see how successful we've been. This, of course, contributes to The Void.

Mental pursuits don't naturally provide the same level of feedback. This has resulted in an emptiness caused by a subconscious realization—that is, we're not sure if we're focused on the most important things. This feeling is compounded by an unfulfilled craving for validation of our efforts.

The Void—an emptiness inside caused by a subconscious realization that we're not sure if we're focused on the most important things.

Coupling the "problem" that it's much easier to meet our basic needs than ever before and the lack of feedback on our actions, many are confused on how to respond. Two options: We can take time to find the cause of The Void and solve our dilemma, or we can take it easy and let modern distractions divert our attention. Given these choices, is it any wonder many have decided to "take it easy"? I have yet to meet more than a handful of people who don't believe they're overwhelmed.

As a natural result, many of us have lost the "fire in the belly" that used to burn. This indicates our lower-order needs have been fulfilled while fulfilling higher order needs (e.g., self-actualization) might not seem possible. Instead of striving to fill The Void in a meaningful way, they feel more comfortable where they are.

Distractions and Lack of Discipline

As a society, we've become prone to *distractions*. Consider the entertainment we "turn on" that replaces more fulfilling pursuits. Hours go by thinking about nothing beyond a sporting event or TV show. We might laugh or cry or feel relieved that, once again, the good guys won—but what did we do in the process? What did we *learn?* How did we *grow?*

Maybe growing up in the military forced me to be more disciplined than most. To make a decision during non-crisis situations required understanding all relevant sides of an issue and discussing options with others. (We expected others to have cogent arguments or we disregarded their opinions. Plus, we didn't lazily subscribe to a preconceived notion about people and their ideas because of a label they wore.) Using this input, we would then decide. Although not all decisions were perfect, most were good.

Is that kind of coordinated discipline lacking in many of our organizations?

In our time *at* work, are we fully engaged *on* work? Productivity falls short when people do activities that have nothing to do with the workplace. So what has our attention? I believe the number one distraction is entertainment.

Countless hours are spent on entertainment—from sports (those we watch, not play), TV shows, social media, movies, interactive video games, and so on. For what gain? Estimates indicate the average American watches five hours of TV each day. That's more than twenty percent of our waking hours! Imagine what we could accomplish if we used just one or two hours of that time on productive activities rather than an escape.

Imagine what we could accomplish if we used just one or two hours of leisure time every day on productive activities rather than an escape.

Face-to-Face Talk

We used to spend more time talking to each other. Have the gains in electronic communication led to a loss of true connection with others? Here's a challenge for you: Find a group of young people talking, not on their cell phones, not texting, but actually talking face to face. To restore my faith in humanity, post a description of your encounter on our KiVisions Facebook page! Maybe that will help.

The young are maligned for these behaviors, but they're not alone. Go to a restaurant and notice how many families spend their entire mealtime using their cell phones. Have we developed an obsession for watching the next installment in others' lives instead of creating new installments in our own? Have these one-way communication issues caused damage to the "feedback loop"? A message should be sent and received, then the receiver provides the sender with feedback. How disengaged do we become when we have no compunction to complete the loop?

Let's look at a few problems that arise because of our obsession with entertainment.

Vicarious Victories

We live vicariously. We even carry our entertainment with us to ensure we don't miss an instant of other people's lives. Plus, too many have adopted a Sports Team Mindset.

Where you live probably has a lot to do with who you root for in professional sports. In my area, most people believe the Steelers, Penguins, and Pirates can do no wrong. No matter how bad our hometown team performs, we'll likely talk "smack" when exchanging pregame guesses with fans from the opposing team.

"Talking Smack"

As the Urban Dictionary (www.urbandictionary.com) offers: To talk trash, insult, or cast doubt.

As humans, we want to be right, so we often take it personally when our team doesn't live up to our expectations, even though few of us have done anything to affect the outcome. By the same token, if our team wins, we celebrate as though we're the sole reason for that victory.

Wanting to experience the pleasure of victory, we often adopt the idea that "any means to the end" is acceptable. What else can explain our forgiveness of the heinous crimes committed by our sports heroes? How does this mindset extend to other facets of our lives?

Escapes, Avatars, and Gaming

Other vicarious quests are related to a need for escape. Listen to the sound track from *The Lord of the Rings* trilogy. Doesn't it evoke a connection to some great quest? But it's a quest we share only vicariously. It's not a real adventure.

In my anecdotal surveys, it's amazing how many people tell me that listening to soundtracks from adventure movies such as *The Lord of the Rings* makes them feel they are right there. They're sharing the adventure with Frodo or Aragorn or Gandalf even though they're sitting comfortably in front of their entertainment centers. Truthfully, the greatest danger in their adventure is the risk of choking on a popcorn kernel.

Many people are even assuming they hold the characteristics of the avatars they've created for games they play.

What is an Avatar?

An avatar combines the Hindu interpretation of the incarnation of a deity and the individual electronic images people build to represent their character in computer games.

The advent of "massively multiplayer online role-playing games (MMORPG)" has had an impact that expands well beyond interactive computer games. It's as though some people believe their avatar is actually more capable in the "real world" than their true self.

Gaming—Good or Bad?

What's your take? Is gaming good or bad? Especially for those who use smart phones, the numbers, types, and constant availability of games has made gaming a national pastime.

Personally, I'm on the fence. Part of me believes gaming is a waste of time, but that impression might be the rationale I use to avoid activities I find addictive. The book *Reality Is Broken* by Jane McGonagle helped me see another side of this—that games are a potential source of fixing our problems. Could they be used as a tool to *unlock, engage, and optimize* human potential? I'd like to explore this.

We're at serious risk, however, if we continue to let the victories of others substitute for our own. If you doubt this, do a reality check. We used to learn from great philosophers. Trust was earned by the influence they had on our ability to understand or do things, not for how they made us feel. A leader development niche is Emotional Intelligence. Do the creators in the entertainment industry understand Emotional Intelligence better than most? After all, our new philosopher "authority figures" have become the star entertainers we watch. Yes, entertainers on the silver screen entertain, but do they have the experience or education to also inform? Do *true* heroes and modern-day philosophers remain unsung as a result?

Apply that logic to what we used to know as the evening "news," which has morphed into editorialized entertainment to compete for viewers. But how are our individual psyches affected by this focus on entertainment? In sports, we demand bragging rights for things we didn't influence. Brag sessions used to occur in the workplace around the water cooler, but in today's spread-out workplace, many have lost this connection place. Emptiness—The Void—results because the feats we speak of aren't our own. More than that, it can create a dangerous mindset of self-indulgence as we feed our vicarious addiction. People who have little to no skin-in-the-game seem likely to adopt an "I Win" Scarcity Mentality as opposed to a shared "We Win" Abundance Mentality.

Although these vicarious behaviors are not classified as criminal, maybe they should be. In my book, it's a crime for anyone to spend their days on time-wasting distractions.

A Lack of Common Goals

This addiction to distraction leads directly to another problem: *a lack of common goals*. Because so many people are watching others, they don't believe they have any responsibility for how things turn out. But how are things really turning out?

For example, one of my students missed a major exam. A few days later, he sent me an email asking how he could make it up. I recommended he come see me during office hours to discuss the situation. It took a while, but he finally did show up and explained he was sick on the day of the exam. I'm no ogre; I've approved many "I was sick" requests.

When I asked for more information, though, this student told me how he got sick. The new iPhone was coming out and he "had to be" one of the first to get one. Wanting to be sure the store didn't run out before he got his new "must have" phone, he camped out in front of it for three days before the sale. Now, where I live, especially during a big part of our school year, the weather isn't conducive to camping. That phone not only caused him to miss an exam but cost him his short-term health. Was it worth it? This case throws light on the damage our addiction to distraction and vicarious living can cause.

Some people may scoff and ask, "How can you get three hundred million people to agree on common goals?" Remember those 5 Key Questions at the beginning of the book? Let's turn to them as goals to pursue. First, no one has been able to dissuade me from these five—not that I've talked to all 300 million people. Second, I don't mean that all 300 million have to agree. I refer to the *most important goals to live by* from which the rest are derived. For example, if my student had felt a shared responsibility for the goal of getting himself successfully through my class, the outcome would have been better for both of us.

It's difficult to find leaders who have the ability to help people understand what good common goals might be and stand behind them. Therefore, we appear to have more people who are going through life with a "whatever" mentality instead of pursuing their purpose.

Scarcity Mentality can also cause the erosion of common goals. People focus on getting more for themselves regardless of their effect on others. Typically, the Scarcity Mentality degrades our overall standard of living and lifestyles. There may be some short-term gains for those who subscribe to it, but over the long run, it hurts much more than helps.

I can't quantify the impact the Sports Team Mindset has on world events except that the problem is oozing into more serious areas of life, including our politics. If we vote for someone only because of party affiliation, our country is likely to cease being a republic and could devolve into a feudal state. If that happens, God help us.

The Danger of Disengagement

The issues outlined here can lead to a serious case of *disengagement*. Sure, people manage to fulfill their "must dos"—but often just enough not to get fired. They are not operating to the best of their ability.

TGIF

As a society, we're so disengaged we've changed the meaning of TGIF. We're no longer **T**hanking **G**od **I**t's **F**riday; we're **T**hanking **G**od **I**t's **F**ive o'clock! Being excited about the end of a difficult workday is nothing new, but for many people, pursuits outside of work could be more fulfilling.

Perhaps we have drifted Off Course because we're losing faith and trust in one another. Many not only disengage from their work but from other people except for superficial reasons. The military culture I lived in, for example, required adoption of an unwritten code of trust. We believed others who held our lives in their hands would do what they said they would do even in the face of death. It's amazing how strong and pervasive that code is. We had faith in each other. Sure, we disagreed with each other on trivial meaningless things. But when it came to serious situations, we believed our comrades-in-arms would have our backs. We were truly engaged with each other.

One way to determine the relative faith I have in people is to note if they use the exploits of others to prop themselves up. I'm frequently dismayed by politicians and journalists who make up stories. Their aim is to make others believe *they* are just as brave as our young men and women who put themselves in harm's way defending this country. This indicates they are disengaged from both a reality and understanding of the damage this does to the psyche of those actually putting their lives on the line defending the country.

Different Generations Different Perspectives

Yes, we have many issues to overcome, and much of the confusion comes from combining in the workplace five distinct generations: Traditionalists, Baby Boomers, Generation X, Generation Y (Millennials), and Generation Z. With so many different perspectives and priorities, how will we ever come together to solve our problems?

This realization is key: We're still all people, and as such, we have similar needs, desires, concerns, and the like. But do we disengage when we don't understand one another rather than try to understand other generations' perspectives?

Dealing with the Generations

The KiVisions Leader Development Process is engineered to help leaders of various generations work well with each other. To get a head start on the issues, follow the writings and work of a generations expert, Lindsey Pollak, at https://www.lindseypollak.com

---

Although our disengagement from the important things may be the ultimate problem society faces, has the fire entirely gone out of our bellies? It appears that too many people are stuck on the ground, not sure what direction to take next. They might be waiting for someone to show them how to better deal with their current circumstances. To reengage requires recognizing the current path is not working. My parents used to tell me (before or after I made some foolish teenage decision), "Ken, you can make any decision you want, as long as you can live with the consequences."

However, if we continue in our distracted, disengaged ways, we'll not only be Off Course but on the Wrong Course. We have the capability to course correct, but first we have to realize the course we're on isn't taking us where we want to go. It's time to grab the controls and learn to become a Great Leader.

An Exciting Time

It's an exciting time to be a leader. Great Leaders are in demand in this new millennium. They can help people Unlock, Engage, and Optimize their potential. Are you ready to become one of those Great Leaders?

---

chapter three
"THE BOSS"—
ABOUT LEADERS

W ho has the single biggest influence on our professional lives? Our bosses. Although most people have more than one boss during their careers, chances are the "boss of the day" has more influence than anyone else right now.

Let me point out two issues about bosses:

✦ Some people think "boss" is a pejorative term. In fact, it has such a negative connotation, I've searched for a more agreeable moniker for those in positions of authority. (I've found none better—but I'm always willing to listen to suggestions.) Until I find a better name, please accept the term "boss." Work to make sure you "Become the Boss *You* Always Wanted" (the second book in our series).

✦ Why are some bosses great and others not so good? Perhaps some believe "the boss" is *supposed to be* an ogre, so they do everything in their power to live up

to that. But a boss's primary function is to be the
kind of facilitator who helps unlock, engage, and
optimize the potential of the people working with
and for him/her. Who wants to be known as an ogre,
a bad boss? My work with bosses makes me believe
many bosses are afraid and simply "fly by the seat of
their pants." Chances are they're not comfortable in
their position of authority. The fear creates a continual
state of tension, which comes through as a negative
attitude toward others. Some bosses attempt to overcome their fear by putting on a show of smug power.
I'm convinced this is an attempt to distance themselves
from subordinates. They hope no one else gets close
enough to realize how afraid they feel.

Most people look to their boss for guidance and hope that person serves well in the role of leader. However, study after study identifies huge disparities between what people in positions of authority
think of their ability to lead and what the people they're supposed to
be leading think of their leadership.

Ongoing Exploration

I began my exploration of bosses with the report *Rewarding
Employees: Balanced Scorecard Fax-Back Survey Result*, published
by William M. Mercer & Co. in 1999. It continues to be sup-
ported by reports such as: "Does the Dunning-Kruger Effect help to explain bad bosses and overrated co-workers?"[2]

Over the past few decades, organizations and individuals have
spent billions on leader development. How successful has this en-

deavor been? I spent many sleepless nights searching for ways to become a good boss, and specifically, a good leader. Unfortunately, the courses and books I explored only painted a picture of what a good leader is *supposed* to be. But nobody explained how to become one.

This book is the first step in a Process designed to help good people become Great Leaders and get to "yes" with the 5 Key Questions from Chapter 1.

Current circumstances require a new model. Our society has evolved technologically, and it's now time to advance the state of the human condition. For that to happen, who will serve as the change catalysts? Leaders.

A Reality Check About Leaders

First, a reality check:

+ There are no perfect leaders. It's rare a person who can put together a perfect day, let alone be a completely perfect leader.

+ The Leader Attribution Theory[3]: One of its multiple facets asserts people often attribute the results of an organization (small or massive) to the leader. The larger an organization gets, however, the likelihood that one person can be held responsible for its success or failure is nonsense. If you are the leader and things go well, I recommend you *not take* all the credit—but, if things go badly and you value integrity, I recommend you *do take* the blame. (This will be explored more deeply and explained in a later book in the series.)

✦ The Law of Attraction is defined this way: By focusing on positive or negative thoughts, people bring positive or negative experiences into their lives. As a leader, you can't just dream or let others just dream, although that's the first step. If I am clear about what I'm looking for (e.g., the resolution to a client's issue, an idea for our leader development series, etc.), I write it down and ponder it. In short order, the answer comes to me. But then I have to *do* something about it.

Definitions of a Leader

Some proclaim the definition of a leader is related to a person's measure of influence. Although there's some truth to this, the concept is too "me" focused. At KiVisions, we define *leader* as *one who shows the way or guides a group of people to a desired outcome*. This definition is more "other" focused, as it needs to be.

Leaders help others establish a clear picture of what they want to achieve—and then help them find and encourage them to take—the action steps necessary to get there.

Still, those who effectively lead others gain plenty of personal rewards.

What Do Leaders Do?

For those they lead, leaders:

1. Envision the intended destination or outcome (explored later in this chapter).

2. Effectively communicate the vision.

3. Unlock the potential and focus the energy of the people working with and for them on accomplishing the mission. "Focus the energy" encompasses both engaging and optimizing human potential.

Caution: True Leaders don't do this in a vacuum.

Whom Do Leaders Lead?

Many people believe leader development is all about learning to lead others. My staff and I know there's a better way, which is why we built the KiVisions Leader Development Process from the ground up. It helps you grow your capability to be a leader through the expected levels of leader readiness. If you do it in this order, your skills will likely be sought after for the rest of your life.

1. First, we'll help you learn to lead *yourself*
2. Then, we'll help you learn to lead others.

Your scope of influence magnifies when you understand how to positively influence the people you are leading indirectly. As a Great Leader, you'll not only have a significant effect on your direct reports, but you'll influence many others, both within and outside of the organization. As people recognize your leadership capabilities, they'll be inclined to follow your lead whether or not you have any direct contact with them.

This is one of the most important reasons to ensure you remain a *True* Leader as you progress to become a Great Leader. Until you can prove your ability to remain On Course, we recommend putting an imaginary "wingman" at every step of your journey.

What is a Wingman?

The true nature of the term *wingman* refers to a position given only to someone flyers will entrust with their lives. Unfortunately, the term has been co-opted by those with more prurient interests. In the terminology of KiVisions, it means someone who will provide support as you become a Great Leader and soar—not score.

What's the prime focus of Great Leaders? As this book title indicates, it's to get us and keep us On Course. Not all leaders achieve this or even intend to achieve it!

Leader Categories

"Leader" is a broad classification, so let's explore basic leader categories. The main characteristic separating the categories of leaders is *vision,* which is why it's part of my company's name.

Vision: what the individual wishes to achieve: for self, the organization, and others in or affiliated with the organization. I will simplify the discussion of vision at this point and only categorize leaders based on whether they are:

+ Helping us derive the vision to stay On Course—**True Leaders.**

+ Causing us to drift Off Course because they haven't taken the time to establish a clear vision —**Wanna-Be Leaders.** (A Wanna-Be is a short version of "wannabe known as, thought of, and rewarded as a True Leader." These individuals typically fall into two classifications:

Either they don't wanna do the work required of a True Leader or they don't yearn to become a True Leader.)

✦ Putting us on the Wrong Course by establishing a vision that primarily serves them —**False Leaders.**

Sound-Bite Descriptors of Leader Types

True Leaders: Role Models

Wanna-Be Leaders: Disingenuous

False Leaders: Dangerous

Leader Qualities

Let's explore a list of leader qualities that goes beyond vision and includes values, responsibility, accountability, value-human-potential, and ownership.

✦ **Values:** As we conduct our Process, we deal with values in each step. We can't address them all at the initial stage of the interview, but here we tackle the most important ones such as integrity, commitment, and focus.

Are Values Always Positive?

People ask, "Are values always positive?" The easy answer is no. The more difficult answer comes with perspective. Many people place value on making a sale, and there's nothing wrong with that. After all, people in business need to be the best salespeople possible.

But in some cases, making a sale can involve actions that degrade any positive value. For example, the seller may focus solely on getting the customer's commitment to "buy" without ensuring that person receives the items stated in the contract. This takes an even darker turn when the seller has *no intention* of delivering those items after closing a deal.

I've witnessed egregious incidents of "false selling" during the hiring/job hunting process. Organizations oversell the benefits of the position, and prospective employees embellish their capabilities beyond reason. The wrong people get hired. What seems like a good idea in the short term can be disastrous long term.

✦ **Responsibility:** True Leaders are responsible adults and expect the people working with and for them to be responsible as well. Here's the reality: If you accept a position of authority, realize you are expected to improve the welfare of the people for whom you are responsible.

✦ **Accountability:** Responsibility and accountability are two sides of the same coin. Accountability ensures responsibility is not just a false promise. I've heard many leaders claim responsibility for a situation, but they assume they don't have to "pay" any other consequences than make the claim. People quickly see through this lack of accountability. It can indicate where a leader stands within the three categories of leader addressed (True, Wanna-Be, or False).

✦ **Value-Human-Potential:** A leader's attitude toward people indicates how much that person *values human potential.* On one end of the spectrum, s/he may believe humans have incredible depths of potential waiting to be unlocked, engaged, and optimized. On the other end of the spectrum, s/he may believe humans are mere commodities whose time, talent, and other resources should be used to serve the leader's needs. When the resources are "used up," the leader may "discard" those people. Note: Where the leader's *attitude* falls on this spectrum can identify the category of that leader (True, Wanna-Be, or False).

✦ **Ownership:** True Leaders know that one way to UEO human potential is to give the people you lead "ownership" of various processes, resources, and so on. It's difficult to do but vital if you want to get back On Course. Ownership generates a personal connection to the outcome, what some call skin-in-the-game. Have you ever had a boss who micro-managed your activities? If so, how did that make you feel? Were you energized to "give your all" in that situation? Probably not.

Let's look at a group—True Leaders—that will hopefully grow in both numbers and capability (remembering no one is perfect).

✦ True Leaders' *Values* are quite consistent; these values start with an Abundance Mentality. For example, True Leaders give credit for a job well done to those involved in the positive outcome (unlike the other categories who are likely to take all the credit for themselves).

✦ Their *Vision* is clear and unifying because they Earnestly Pursue their Purpose with Passion—and their Purpose helps determine their Vision.

✦ Their sense of *Responsibility* is demonstrated by concentrating on Priorities, Their work ethic gets the job done; they maintain the group's focus on the Vision; they continually strive to improve, especially in their role as leader.

✦ They show *Accountability* by ensuring the group stays On Course. They are quick to make necessary adjustments and willing to admit mistakes (usually in a way that helps everyone learn and ensures the mistakes don't recur).

✦ Some leaders claim to *Value Human Potential,* but then they fail to use that potential. These are not True Leaders. True Leaders help crew members believe they have a proper level of *Ownership* for the various processes and resources for which they have responsibility.

Note: The Table of Qualities and Clarifying Questions in Appendix B provides an overview of how individuals in each leader category think and function.

True Leaders recognize people are hired to fulfill a function. First, they make sure people working with and for them have what they need to do the job. Then they work with them to go even deeper into that limitless "well" of human potential.

Role of Charisma

The quality called charisma is terribly misleading. Although there's nothing wrong with charisma, you can't rely on it to characterize the full value of a leader. Too many people place instant credibility on leaders who exude charisma and discount others who do not. Both judgments are a mistake. Humans have always been suckers for a great orator. The problem has become even worse in our current "entertainment society" where charisma has been elevated to a level much higher than most other qualities. Be cautious of those who instantly capture your attention. Make them prove their bona-fides in the other qualities noted before you "buy" what they're "selling."

Leader Types and Depressing Issues

With respect to the people working with and for them, let's look at how each type of leader deals with one of the most depressing issues people face: feelings of helplessness and frustration.

True Leaders strive to turn these feelings to joy and fulfillment through the achievements of the people working with and for them so they can accomplish their goals under the True Leaders' tutelage.

Wanna-Be Leaders often use "helping others deal with their issues" as a means to get others to "owe them." Other Wanna-Be's pretend to lead, mainly because they either have trouble seeing things clearly or don't want to do the work. If a situation makes them look bad, they make others pay them back by serving as scapegoats when needed.

False Leaders are energized by others' problems and situations. These types of issues "stoke their fires" as they learn about others' fears. They use those fears to accomplish what they want with little regard to what others get out of the situation. They simply don't care.

The Peter Principle

What about those thrown into a leadership position with little preparation, training, or development? This may have happened to you or someone you know. If so, you know how problematic the situation can be because you or that person didn't ask for the leadership position. Others ask for or end up in leadership positions well before they're ready. This is when the Peter Principle comes into play. It happens more often than desirable!

This principle stems from the assumption that because someone was a good engineer, salesperson, physician, and so on, s/he will automatically be good in a position requiring leadership, with no development necessary. It was formulated by Laurence J. Peter, a Canadian educator who wrote a book by the same name, *The Peter Principle: Why Things Always Go Wrong.* (See Appendix D.) For those frustrated by their current work situation, the book just might provide comic relief as well as confirmation on how some people find themselves in positions for which they are not qualified.

Alive and Well

For almost forty years, I worked for two large hierarchies and can attest that, in many cases, the Peter Principle is alive and well. Although it doesn't happen 100 percent of the time, many situations prove how true it can be. Before people get promoted into a position of authority, bear consideration to the Peter Principle. Through the years, I've experienced many of its victims, both the unqualified leaders and those they led. The unqualified leaders weren't in a position of authority because of their proven capability as leaders— and I was among them. When I transitioned from flying to

---

running medical centers, I faced no "test" to determine my fitness to lead; it was assumed I would do okay. Yet I'd been promoted into a position of authority based on my excellence as a flyer, not a leader. Dr Peter could have used me as an example for his work!

Too many people have suffered due to poor leadership from unqualified, untrained bosses. Key point: Don't assume someone's proficiency in a technical area automatically qualifies that person to be a leader.

A Decision to Make

Those who find themselves in this predicament have a decision to make: Learn how to be a True Leader *quickly* or suffer the negative consequences. The biggest obstacle to this issue is ego. As my coaching clients have told me, "But I was good at what I was doing before I accepted this position. Why do I suck at being a leader?" My response is: "I get it. I was there, too. That's why I can help—because I suffered as I figured it out. The good news is I want to share a solution with as many leaders as possible. It starts by adopting the True Leaders Code."

The True Leader's Code

"I will be *dauntless*. I will do what needs to be done, by when it needs to be done, in a manner consistent with my values, especially on days I don't feel up to it. Many people are counting on me to fulfill my calling, my purpose, my mission."

Being a True Leader isn't the easiest job in the world, but it is one of the most important. It requires us to start each day with courage in our hearts and, while looking in the mirror, recite the True Leader's Code.

After you recite the Code each morning, go make it happen. It's true: If you are a leader, many are counting on you to fulfill your calling, your purpose, and your mission.

True Leaders also recognize they can make a positive difference by including the entire "crew" in achieving the vision of the organization. This aspect of "ownership" shows in their deep desire to unlock, engage, and optimize the potential in all their crewmembers.

Historical Examples of Leadership

In addition to the sound-bite characteristics offered earlier for each leader category, here are three historical examples of each type. Remembering there are no perfect leaders, the examples are:

True Leader: Winston Churchill—served as prime minister of Great Britain during World War II. His country served a critical role in removing the threat of world domination by the Nazis. During this brutal period, Mr. Churchill performed magnificently in keeping the British people positive and focused, despite the hardships they endured. His actions during WWII exemplified those of a True Leader.

Wanna-Be Leader: Neville Chamberlain—Great Britain's prime minister for the period leading up to and at the beginning of WWII. Like many Wanna-Be Leaders, Mr. Chamberlain assumed his charisma would be the magic that would "win the day" over the tyrant Adolph Hitler. Mr. Chamberlain was probably a fun guy to go have a beer with but proved to be over matched in his role as leader of one of the key countries during wartime.

False Leader: Adolf Hitler—Chancellor of Germany in the lead-up to and during WWII. He too used charisma as a key to establishing his power. He mesmerized audiences but was ruthless in his use of power to achieve his personal vision.

Why did I place Churchill and Chamberlain where I did? (I doubt anyone will challenge me on categorizing Adolf Hitler as a False Leader.) To explain, read these excerpts from three speeches and attempt to determine which of these men gave each speech.

Speech #1: "We regard the agreement signed last night...as symbolic of the desire of our two peoples never to go to war with one another again. We are resolved that the method of consultation shall be the method adopted to deal with any other questions that may concern our two countries, and we are determined to continue our efforts to remove possible sources of difference, and thus to contribute to assure the peace...My good friends, this is the second time in our history that there has come...peace with honor. I believe it is peace for our time."

Speech #2: "In this crisis I hope I may be pardoned if I do not address the House at any length today. I hope that any of my friends and colleagues, or former colleagues, who are affected by the political reconstruction, will make all allowances for any lack of ceremony with which it has been necessary to act. I would say to the House, as I said to those who have joined this government, I have nothing to offer but blood, toil, tears, and sweat. We have before us an ordeal of the most grievous kind. We have before us many, many long months of struggle and of suffering. You ask, what is our policy? I can say: It is to wage war, by sea, land, and air, with all our might and with all the strength that God can give us; to wage war against a monstrous tyranny, never surpassed in the dark, lamentable catalog of human crime. That is our policy. You ask, what is our aim? I can answer in one word: Victory. Victory at all costs, victory in spite of all terror, victory however long and hard the road may be. For without victory, there is no survival. Let that be realized…"

Speech #3: "When appointing men to leading positons… greater value should be placed on character than on purely academic or allegedly intellectual suitability. It is not abstract knowledge which must be considered as a decisive factor wherever a leader is required but rather a natural talent for leadership, and with it a highly developed sense of responsibility which brings with it determination, courage, and endurance. It must be recognized on principle that the lack of a sense of responsibility can never be made up for by a supposedly first-class academic training, of which certificates may supply the fruit. Knowledge and qualities of leadership, which always imply energy, are not incompatible. But in doubtful cases knowledge can in no circumstances be a substitute for integrity, courage, bravery and determination. These are the qualities that are more important in a leader of the people . . ."

Without looking them up, can you guess which speech our three "gentlemen" delivered? Unless you've listened to them or studied them, you might be surprised to understand who gave each one.

Speech #1 was delivered by Neville Chamberlain, who truly believed his charisma and prowess won Hitler over and the risk of war had been averted by his "diplomacy." This was shortly before Adolf Hitler proved how untrustworthy he was as he marched his armies into Czechoslovakia (prior to the Czech Republic and Slovakia becoming separate nations). But leadership has little to do with likability. Chamberlain might have been a fun guy to hang around with, but as a leader, he left a lot to be desired. The sad reality is he was responsible for more pain and suffering than would have likely occurred if a True Leader had been in his position.[4]

Leadership has little to do with likability.

Speech #2 sounds warlike and seems unlikely to have been given by a True Leader. Well, True Leaders do their best to view reality with their eyes wide open—to see things as they are, not as they and others want them to be. They're not willing to allow good people to be destroyed by a sense of false peace.

True Leaders do their best to view reality with their eyes wide open—to see things as they are, not as they and others want them to be.

This speech was delivered by Winston Churchill. Without him, the British probably wouldn't have been able to hold on long enough for the United States to become involved. Churchill, like all of us, had his flaws and foibles. But he was a True Leader.[5]

Does your impression of Hitler match the verbiage in Speech #3? Maybe not—but yes, this was delivered by Adolf Hitler. He presents another case of problems caused by using charisma or force of personality in leadership—although his charisma was not positive. It's typical of many False Leaders to be "wolves in sheep's clothing," but some have been obvious "wolves."[6]

A number of False Leaders have been worse than Hitler, especially if we consider the deaths that resulted due to their "leadership." Lenin, Stalin, Mao, and Pol Pot certainly make the list. (Pol Pot wouldn't make this list in terms of numbers of deaths but certainly would considering the percentage of the Cambodian people who died as a result of his decrees.) Note: If these names are unfamiliar to you, take time to research their roles in world history.

Wish Fulfillment: Left Hand, Right Hand Concept

Have you heard the expression "If wishes were horses, then beggars would ride"? Wishes are ubiquitous, but we need to establish a clear and deliberate vision, then work to make the vision come true. And as leaders, it's our responsibility to see things as they are, not as we want them or wish them to be. Remember, this was one of Churchill's strong points as a True Leader.

The Left Hand, Right Hand concept is fairly simple. Hold out your hands with your palms facing upward. While looking into your left palm, wish for something you want to come true. While you wish, *real life* is filling up your right hand. Will your wishes come true? They can—through a clear vision, a realistic understanding of the situation, and hard work. But you can't sit around expecting things will happen just because you wished for them. Your right hand will fill up quickly while your wishes languish in your left hand.

The key to the Left Hand, Right Hand concept is to make sure you know what you want (the purpose of "visioning") and then put a plan into action. By this time, you may be thinking, "It seems as if being a True Leader is difficult." Yes, it does take a lot of work, and maybe you don't want to be a True Leader. But being such a leader doesn't require you to be a Winston Churchill.

Name True Leaders in Your Life

Like me, you've probably had many True Leader "bosses" in your life. Who are those influencers and True Leaders? How can you become one? And once you are a True Leader, how can you become a Great Leader?

Abundance vs. Scarcity Mentality

Your path to becoming a True Leader and then a Great Leader requires developing an Abundance Mentality. I learned this concept from Dr. Stephen Covey who wrote *The 7 Habits of Highly Effective People.* (I was certified as a facilitator in his "7 Habits" program many years ago.)

The idea is to lean toward "We Win" as opposed to "I Win." Those with an "I Win" focus have a Scarcity Mentality in which the objective in every engagement with others is a triumph over others. "I Win" people work to ensure they get the best deal, regardless of the effects on others. In contrast, people with an Abundance Mentality take a mature, transformational approach and have a "We Win" focus.

Which are you? Be honest and realistic in your appraisal of yourself because the people you are intended to lead will likely follow your behaviors and adopt your mentality. Which mentality would you prefer the people in your organization adopt?

Asked another way, how would you like to work in an organization in which everyone was out for himself or herself? A day will come when you need others—who may not support you if you behave from a Scarcity Mentality. If you haven't helped them, why would they be there to help you?

Tuning in to the Right Stations

I love music and, whenever possible, I have tunes playing in the background while I work. I suggest adding a couple of "stations" with the call letters WIFM and WCIC.

WIFM is the acronym for "What's In it For Me?" Many including Dr. Covey recognized the need to take care of yourself: To grow from the Dependent to the Independent stage; to achieve Private Victory by Being Proactive; to Begin with the End in Mind; and to Put First Things First.[7] That said, as we move to the more mature stage of Public Victory, we're asked to think Win-Win. How? By establishing an Abundance Mentality, which assures us there's plenty "out there" for all.

The Abundance Mentality plays through the station WCIC: "What Can I Contribute?" This station requires you to understand that everyone has something grand inside just waiting to come out. What is inside *you* that could make your life and the rest of the world much better?

If you want to accomplish your goals and Unlock, Engage, and Optimize the human potential in your organization, first adopt an Abundance Mentality.

Where do you fall along the "I Win" to "We Win" spectrum? Reflect on the magnitude of what you've done to help your crew (not only yourself) achieve one or more goals. If in doubt, ask people who work with or for you. Hopefully, the environment you've set allows them to feel comfortable giving you an honest answer.

You won't find either station WIFM or WCIC online, but you can hear more about them and many of the other topics in this book and on the "Better Bosses Blog" at www.KiVisions.com.

A "We Win" Example

Herb Heilbrun flew B-17s in World War II. As you can imagine, this was a highly dangerous job. Out of the 12,000 B-17s that were built, the Nazis shot down more than 4,500 of them. The strategists decided that to protect these bombers striving to diminish Nazi capability, they would assign fighter squadrons to defend the bombers as they approached target areas. But many of these fighter pilots got "distracted" by the chance to earn greater status if they shot down the Nazi fighters targeting our bombers. Some Nazi units recognized that when the fighters chased one or more of their fighter planes, the bombers were left unprotected. They began to assign "decoy" status to some of their fighters in the hopes our fighter protection squadrons would be drawn away from our bombers. Even though some of our fighter pilots reveled in the personal glory of shooting down a Nazi fighter, the results weren't beneficial to our war effort.

John Leahr was a member of the famous Tuskegee Airmen. He and other pilots flying P-51s (one of the best fighter planes of all time) were assigned to guard Heilbrun's squadron. This is significant for two reasons. First, the Tuskegee Airmen were recognized as having a "We Win" mentality. The indignities they suffered could have easily caused them to go after personal glory rather than protect these bombers filled with "white" crewmembers, but they did not. Of those 4,500 B-17s shot down, the total lost while being protected by Tuskegee Airmen equaled zero—*yes, zero!*

Out of the many stories I could have picked, why Herb and John? Unknown to either man at the time they were flying their missions, Heilbrun and Leahr had been grade-school classmates at North Avondale School in Cincinnati when they were eight years old.

The lesson: It's amazing what people can do when they work together for the common good and demonstrate an Abundance ("We Win") Mentality.

Become an ACE

The best way to grow an organization large or small is to become an ACE:

1. Adopt and live with the Abundance Mentality,

2. Concentrate on Priorities, and

3. Earnestly Pursue your Purpose with Passion—putting as much heart, mind, body, and soul into something as possible.

To better understand the definition of passion, let me insert the concept of suffering. For example, I'm intensely passionate about helping good people become Great Leaders, but getting to this point has been anything but peaceful or easy. I've had to overcome untold obstacles and endless doubts. Was it worth it? Yet the more people I help, the fewer doubts I have and the more fulfilled I feel.

You, too, may suffer as you work your way along the True Leader path, but if this type of leadership becomes your passion, the joys will overwhelm the pain.

Younger Generations

Almost daily, I read indicators that many people in the younger generations want to be part of something bigger than themselves.[8] They might gravitate to this True Leader mindset if we give them a chance and show them how to achieve it. This training also might help combat the problem of disloyalty that many organizations experience with some young members of their crews. (We deal with this topic in another book in our series.)

But we have a dilemma to resolve: Becoming an ACE is atypical to the current human condition. ACEs need to take the path less traveled. Who is going to lead the transformation? Who will support them?

These questions imply we need lots of good people to become Great Leaders so they can help people UEO their potential and fulfill their dreams.

chapter four
THE FRAMEWORK OF THE KIVISIONS LEADER DEVELOPMENT PROCESS

I n the past, the "command and control" style of leadership (i.e., I say, you do) was the only one deemed useful. About the time I was first asked to be a boss (1982), Organizational Behaviorists were starting to "roll out" new ideas. Unfortunately, I was using the standard "command and control" style. The early results showed that my "crew":

+ wasn't inspired

+ wasn't making much progress

+ had horribly ineffective systems

+ had too much deadweight

+ was constantly bombarded by issues beyond our control.

I set off on a quest to overcome the obstacles and discover the solution, but I struggled to find the help I needed. The courses, books, and seminars I took proposed what a good leader should be but never laid out a plan for how to become one. As Albert Einstein offered, "Insanity is doing the same thing over and over again and expecting different results." That told me good people striving to become great leaders needed a new way. Because I could find nothing that resolved my concerns, I came to believe the answer might have to come from me. Many sleepless nights followed.

I started by reflecting on my past. I'd had some jobs I loved and some I hated. I wondered why there was such disparity until I realized my boss made all the difference. S/he either made the experience positive and worthwhile or negative and wishing I was doing anything else. Because of that, I set my sights on becoming the best boss I could be.

After achieving consistent progress (measured by the results my "crews" achieved), I began to focus on a new quest: *help others achieve similar success*. To me, this meant solving the single most important mystery for leaders: *how best to unlock, engage, and optimize human potential*. What I now believe is the essence of leading. I reflected on the things that were missing from everything I had tried—many of them frustrating. To minimize the frustration during their journey and help them become Great Leaders, I came up with these three focal points while developing the Process:

1. Make it simple to understand so the average person who wants to lead can achieve success.

2. Provide a pictorial representation to serve as a frame of reference when leaders are faced with an issue to resolve (e.g., learning from past situations, contemplat-

ing the best course for current issues, and deliberating future plans).

3. Ensure it can be easily recalled so it will be functional in all arenas.

The epiphany I shared earlier—"Could it be that what it takes to get an organization off the ground is similar to what it takes to get an airplane off the ground?"—led me to develop the model that would improve the decisions made by leaders. An early version of this model helped me achieve a turnaround in the results my crews and I experienced. After testing and refining, I landed on the model all True Leaders could use to become Great Leaders: the Successful Ventures in Human Dynamics Model™.

The Successful Ventures in Human Dynamics Model

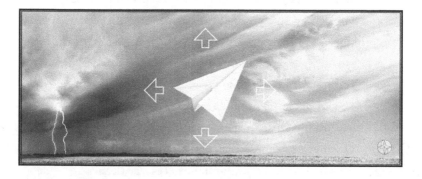

The Model recognizes that what it takes to get an aircraft or an organization "off the ground and to its destination" are amazingly similar. The *plane* in the Model represents a number of possible focal points including you, your "crew", organization, etc. The "paper airplane" is intended to help you realize the Model works for all leaders. Regardless of the size or type of organization, the factors and dynamic motion are the same. The differences are in the scale and scope of the operations. Now, a brief look at each Step in the Model:

1. The plane must be pointed toward the desired destination and

2. Properly "outfitted" to accomplish the mission/ achieve the vision.

   (Understanding the impact and effectively using the four "forces" below will help you become a better leader. The key: As a leader, you must balance these forces to ensure the organization achieves its goals. No force is necessarily positive, no force is necessarily negative.)

3. *Lift* (represented by the up arrow) gives you the *potential* to "get off the ground." Lift is primarily created by what inspires and helps each person derive the motivation to achieve the organization's Vision and Mission. The caveat: If you aren't careful, you might "go too high." The higher you go, requires greater mastery and usually more sophisticated and expensive equipment. Too much "height" might cause you to lose perspective. The adage "can't see the forest for the trees" implies you are too close to the situation to see the big picture. The inverse can also be true; you might be too far from the situation to understand the necessary details.

4. *Thrust* (represented by the arrow facing right) propels you forward and allows *potential* lift to become *actual* lift. Thrust is primarily created by coordinated individual, "crew," and/or group efforts producing effective results. The caveat: If you aren't careful, you might "go too fast." So work to ensure you are ready for full

throttle before you stress yourself and your "plane" beyond limits. I've seen organizations develop a great product and market it effectively, but they do this well before they are ready to meet the demand created.

5. ***Drag*** (represented by the arrow facing left), primarily caused by ineffectiveness that holds you back. In my experience, people communicating poorly, especially when they miscommunicate, is the single biggest cause of drag. It indicates the "parts" aren't working well together. Think about people new to the organization who need to learn how things work. The caveat: Being "held back" can be a good thing. That's why most organizations need a Devil's Advocate to ensure the what/when/how/why/where have been carefully considered.

Devil's Advocate

A Devil's Advocate is a person who expresses a contentious opinion meant to provoke debate or test the strength of the opposing arguments.

If you're uncomfortable infusing debate into your organization, you need to overcome that if you want to succeed. In his book *5 Dysfunctions of a Team*, Patrick Lencioni identifies Fear of Conflict as one of the major dysfunctions in organizations today. Too many assume that all conflict must be "resolved" and that all conflict is dysfunctional. But that's just not true.

In the "going too fast" situation noted, an effective Devil's Advocate would have made sure the leader(s) of that organization had contemplated all aspects before marketing the product to customers.

6. *Weight* (represented by the down arrow) makes it harder to "get off the ground and climb." All weight is inevitably affected by *gravity,* discussed later as an External Condition. Dead Weight, which is potential that's "locked up" in humans, is a key issue for leaders to resolve. It indicates a lack of a clear vision and mission or the crew's connection to both. The caveat: As the saying goes, being "grounded in reality" can be a good thing. The sports industry offers solid analogies for business. For example, *Hoosiers* is one of my favorite movies, primarily because it's based on real-life events.[9] Although many "liberties" were taken in the creation of the movie, the actual story includes incidents that relate to our discussion. Compare the skills, experience, and depth of the teams of the schools that played in the Indiana State Championship game in 1954: Milan High School Indians ("Hickory" in the movie) and the Muncie Central Bearcats ("South Bend" in the movie). The differences are stark. Muncie should have won easily. It is my opinion that the Muncie coaches and team saw their pre-game chances against Milan as an easy victory and didn't play to their potential. It shows leaders must be careful to remain grounded in reality regardless of what appearances indicate. You want to UEO the potential in your organization!

(As a leader, you have some measure of control, or at least influence, over the "plane you fly" {i.e., you or the organization} and each of the four *forces* identified here. No force is necessarily positive; no force is necessarily negative. The key: As a leader, you must balance these forces to ensure the organization achieves its goals.

7. *External Conditions* (primarily represented by the
    storm) are the issues over which you have little, if any,
    control or influence, as these examples show.

    a. Some External Conditions are obstacles you need
        to avoid. A flying example: The storm depicted
        in the model is a natural obstacle and dangerous
        to fly through. Organizations encounter many
        "storms," such as competing products that un-
        expectedly take market share and customers who
        change their expectations of price, quality, delivery
        times, and so on. Your organization might have
        some conditions that are similar to others, but you
        are also likely to have conditions that are specific
        to your situation. Be sure you have a clear idea of
        which conditions to avoid and then take necessary
        actions to do so.

    b. Other External Conditions can't be avoided; you
        need to deal with them. For flyers, wind is unavoid-
        able; not only is it always present, the direction
        and velocity change frequently affecting take-offs,
        navigation, and more. Many External Conditions
        such as changes in regulations can seriously disrupt
        current processes. They will also likely affect your
        organizational plans and outcomes.

Whether you're dealing with a simple organization or growing a
conglomerate, all the forces affecting an organization are interconnected. A change in one force affects the others. Just as a good flyer
properly balances an airplane, your job as leader is to keep these
forces in balance.

> ### Decisions Leaders Make
>
> Although the Successful Ventures in Human Dynamics Model has potentially broad implications, the KiVisions Leader Development Process focuses on the decisions the leaders of an organization make that relate to people, systems, and structures.

Myths of Leadership

Many myths about leadership cause significant problems and can hold you back or throw you off course. Let's look at a few and see how they relate to the model:

1. "I'm a leader because I'm in a leadership position." The statement itself is true but assuming you're in this position because of your leadership skills is a common myth that causes some of the biggest problems. The people who put you in the position of authority expect you to achieve results. But don't be fooled into believing they measured your ability to lead and that's why you were put into the position. As discussed with the Peter Principle, relative proficiency in one position is a prime reason people are elevated to leadership positions. But the proficiency in some technical field does not necessarily qualify you to lead well. True Leader status will only be granted after you have proven yourself capable to the people on your crew. A tip: Your success as a True Leader depends on your ability to achieve good results *with* your crew members, not at their expense.

I recommend you begin using the Model and learning from your experiences, especially your mistakes.

2. "I can't be a leader because . . :

   a. "I'm not in a leadership position." I guarantee you are a leader in some aspect of your life. As we work through the Process, you'll find the best organizations are full of leaders, not just people "at the top." As mentioned previously, ownership is a key aspect leaders should relegate to the people working with them. Taking ownership of something within your area of responsibility requires you to lead. You, too, can use the Model for this purpose. It will provide a great experience if you choose to accept a leadership position in the future.

   OR

   b. "I don't know how." The answer to the age-old question "are leaders made or born?" is *yes*. There are some people who seem to have natural gifts that help them lead well. Regardless, I have worked with enough people who initially had few leader skills. A large number of them became highly capable leaders. I guarantee you can learn to lead if you sincerely commit to the effort.

3. "Because I'm good at _____ (fill-in-the-blank), I'll also be a good leader." Remember the Peter Principle discussed earlier? Unfortunately, there's *no* guarantee that because you are good at _____ (fill-in-the-blank), you will also be a good leader. I was living proof. My performance evaluations indicated I was good at flying

and then handling the technical aspects of running medical centers. Did this mean I'd be a good leader? Not so much. I had to work hard at it. The good news: Having the right attitude, working hard on developing my skills, and using the Model, I became a much better leader. Using the same process, I am confident you too can achieve stunning results.

4. "I'm as successful as I'm going to get because I'm too busy to find a better way." Newsflash! We all have the same number of hours in a day. Over time, you can learn to use your hours differently to be more effective, not just busy. Plus, many give this excuse for not being the leader they'd like to be because they don't know where to turn to get the help they need. But now you know where to turn. Start by employing the Model and learning from your experiences. In his 7 Habits book, Dr. Covey related a story about the wood cutter who becomes dismayed that his productivity is decreasing. When his boss asks, "When was the last time you sharpened your axe?" the man replies, "Sharpen? I had no time to sharpen my axe. I have been very busy trying to cut trees." Although sharpening often helps, it isn't always the best course of action. As it relates to helping good people become great leaders, sometimes the "axe" needs to be replaced. That's what I did when I started using the Model to become a better leader.

5. "I can be, do, and have everything I want." Perhaps you've never said this, but do your actions imply you believe it? Deep down, you know it's not possible. One reason ACE is addressed before the Model is to ensure you are concentrating on priorities.

6. "Leaders must be born with the necessary attributes. I don't think I have them so there's no sense even trying." The corollary to this one is "My _____ (fill-in-the-blank with your favorite relative) was a Great Leader, so I must have the same attributes." Is this always the case for familial monarchies? How do they turn out? The same bloodline has produced both good monarchs and lousy ones. I think many people use this as an excuse because, like me in the beginning of my leader experiences, I didn't know where to turn for the answers. That's why I spent thirty years developing the KiVisions Leader Development Process to help you become a Great Leader. No more excuses!

7. "Leadership is merely a buzzword." If you believe this, I hope you'll soon realize the importance of true leadership and how powerful it can be.

Only you know if one or more of these myths has affected your ability to lead. Do your best to work through them and overcome any problems.

Why Use the Model?

Using the Successful Ventures in Human Dynamics Model will help you achieve a degree of success and provide the satisfaction that makes you want to be even better.

As I was testing the use of the Model early on, I found I needed more structure and began exploring how to best serve those who wanted to grow their capability. One realization came from some of the courses I attempted. They had a "one-size-fits-all" framework, and probably because I was a fairly new leader, this realization hit me hard. I was working with people senior to me who naturally grasped concepts that didn't match my experiences. Because of that, it became imperative to work with people at their level of leader readiness and offer the tools needed to serve leaders throughout their journey. After some experimentation, I centered on three levels: Emerging Leaders, Leaders with History, Leaders of Leaders.

Emerging Leaders: It's hard to determine when this level starts (out of the womb?), but we assume it starts when a person takes on a Position of Authority (POA). The process to "graduate" to the next level typically takes ten years or so and assumes the Emerging Leader goes through three phases: 1) gains credibility and becomes known for competence in some "field"—usually technical, not leadership, 2) seeks to develop a rudimentary understanding of what a leader is and does, and 3) tests the waters by applying leader techniques to the requirements of the POA. Some leaders are ready to "graduate" earlier than others; some need more than ten years at the level of Emerging Leader.

Leaders with History: It usually requires 10 years of experience in POA before someone has the depth and breadth of experiences to cross into this level. One critical aspect of the Leader with History is a person's cognitive acceptance of the need to develop the people they're responsible for.

Leaders of Leaders: This level typically requires twenty years of experience in POA. The key demarcation for this level is being able and willing to develop people at both of the previous levels. It is a difficult facet of a senior leader because it requires the ability to comprehend the level of readiness of junior leaders. Wise leaders accept the finite period of their leadership role and do everything they can to leave the organization in good hands when it's time for the senior leader to accept new challenges.

Applying a clear understanding of the levels of leader readiness, I had to build the material that would support leadership develop-ment at each level. But because the length of the process might span a leader's entire professional career, it became clear that, like the U.S. Air Force, I should build in a mechanism to incentivize people to reach ever higher levels of capability. Today, I challenge all leaders and provide opportunities to earn "Ratings" that signify their level of leader proficiency. Here are the ratings:

+ *Earn Your Wings.* This is oriented toward helping Emerg-ing Leaders fully grasp the importance of managing expectations. Plus, it gives senior leaders a baseline for developing Emerging Leaders.

+ *Master Flight.* Oriented toward helping Leaders with History consistently achieve excellence. Plus, it gives more senior leaders a baseline for developing Leaders with History.

+ *Soar:* Oriented toward developing Leaders of Leaders. It is the pinnacle rating for Great Leaders wishing to achieve and sustain exceptional results. It also serves as an extraordinary succession planning primer.

But just as I didn't walk out on the flight-line, have someone throw me the "keys to the airplane," and take off, leaders at all lev-els must start with a framework for effective growth. I developed Ground School to serve as the Foundational Complement that pro-vides this framework.

On Course Sets the Tone for Ground School

This book *On Course* provides the foundational information required by Ground School.

Because flyers have a responsibility to Maintain Currency, I built that option into the KiVisions Leader Development Process as well. As another Complement, it is intended to supplement each Rating by helping leaders maintain a path toward greater competency within the Rating they have earned.

The next challenge was to build the content necessary for leader growth. Our *Helping True Leaders Soar to Greatness* leader development series unlocks the secrets of the Successful Ventures in Human Dynamics Model, educates leaders at their level of readiness, and supports the Rating/Complement challenge outlined above.

9 Phases in the Helping True Leaders Soar to Greatness Series™

Here are the phases in the series and the Rating/Complement each supports:

✦ To support *Ground School:*

Phase 1: "On Course: How Good People Become Great Leaders"

✦ To support Earn Your Wings:

Phase 2: "Become the Boss You Always Wanted"

Phase 3: "The Leader's Magic Mirror" (2 parts):

First Look: Your Internal REFLECTION

Second Take: Your External IMAGE

Phase 4: "Lead with PRIDE."

✦ To support *Master Flight:*

Phase 5: "True Leaders Grow Forward"

Phase 6: "The Leader's Path: From the Ideal, through the Ordeal, to the Real Deal"

Phase 7: "The Leader's 'Investment' Tool: Ken's IRA"

✦ To support *Soar:*

Phase 8: "Make Your Organization CLICK."

✦ To support *Maintain Currency:*

Phase 9: _____ (Built as necessary to keep you Growing Forward)

(You'll find an outline of the KiVisions Leader Development Process in Appendix A at the back of this book.)

The Gyroscope System

In addition to the Successful Ventures in Human Dynamics Model, I incorporated the components that will support your development into another visual representation: Our Gyroscope System.

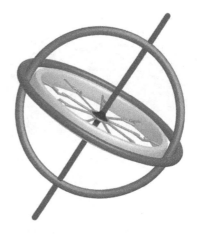

The KiVisions *Gyroscope System*

The Gyroscope speaks to the intent of the Process in the business world. An integral component in all modern aircraft, gyros are incredibly useful for maintaining orientation. Our Gyroscope System helps you, your crew, your organization, and more get from where you are to where you want to be. (You can watch a video that explains how all the pieces of the Gyroscope System fit together on our website, www.KiVisions.com)

Now that you have a better understanding of the KiVisions Leader Development Process, let's get On Course by pointing your "plane" in the desired direction.

chapter five
ENVISIONING THE DESTINATION

The most important skill you need to hone to become a Great Leader is vision—i.e., determining which direction to point your "plane." As it relates to your organization or you as an individual, vision means knowing the best direction to go.

As a wise soul once taught me, *your vision is like the horizon; you should always be headed toward it, but never reach it.* You'll always have something more out in front of you. It may be this abstract nature of vision that keeps so many people from becoming Great Leaders. They need something more tangible. But you can start by discerning the result you want. As Dr. Covey taught, "Begin with the end in mind."

What problem do you want to solve or situation do you want to improve?

When I first became a boss, I wanted to know how I could be a better leader, so I set out to solve that problem. This led me to realize the Model I created could serve a bigger purpose—that is, helping other leaders achieve greater success. Today, I have yet to reach my horizon for there's always something more to achieve. I'll continue to help good people become Great Leaders until I no longer want to "extend the horizon." My guess is, I will die before that happens.

Vision Test

Perhaps people need a Vision Test before they're placed in a position of authority.

WHERE
SHOULD
YOU & YOUR
ORGANIZATION
BE HEADED?
WHAT MAKES
YOU THINK
YOU CAN
GET THERE?

To understand your own vision, ask these two questions:

1. Where should you and your organization be headed?
2. What makes you think you can get there?

Don't pick a direction because it sounds good. Make sure it's the right direction and best path for you.

Almost Like Cheating

Caution: Notice the Vision Test gets "fuzzy" as the letters get smaller. *Our Vision Test Cheat Sheet* (the Operational Focus Tool we'll explore in a bit) can shave off twenty-plus years of learning. It's almost like cheating.

When developing vision, it boils down to this: *Will you make good decisions today that will still be good decisions tomorrow?* Make sure you can prove your answer to this question based on your track record. It's easy to claim you've made good decisions, but can you prove it based on your long-term results? Would those who have worked with and for you agree with your assessment?

Here's a saying that keeps me humble: "It's not that people can't solve their own problems, it's that they can't SEE their own problems." (I wish I could properly attribute this to the original author. I first heard this in a seminar years ago but didn't think much of it until I started helping people resolve their problems.) Even the most poorly run organization likely has the ability to serve a purposeful function if the leaders are willing to open their eyes and see clearly.

Decisions, Decisions

During one of KiVisions' seminars, a person who had been in positions of authority for twenty-plus years, asked, "Are we discussing leadership or decision-making?" Let's be clear: Everything leaders do is because of decisions they have made or will make, consciously or not.

Start by ensuring that your direction (as indicated by your vision) is clear and deliberate. When you set your vision, you aren't merely asking people to go along for a ride. You're asking them to contribute to the best of their ability. You're affecting yourself and many other people, as well. As you set your direction, consider the impact it will have on others.

Vision Issues

Consider the following Vision Issues before you start your exploration.

- **No Joy.** This is a term combat flyers learn early. It's typically used in the KiVisions Leader Development Process when someone else (usually a Wingman) identifies an issue and brings it to your attention. Often, we attempt to verify the issue due to our limitations as humans. When we can't visualize or understand it, we call "No Joy." This indicates we need help with something.

  Ahh, hard on the ego, eh? But don't take the need to call "No Joy" as an offense or failure. Those mature enough to call "No Joy" often "live to fly another day." There's nothing wrong with admitting you need help.

- **Distortions and Distractions.** One of the tools used to explore space is the telescope. When the innovative Hubble telescope was built, instead of being terrestrial-based, it was launched into space. Why? Because of the need to remove distractions and distortions caused by the atmosphere.

  Similarly, it helps to remove the normal day-to-day distractions that keep you from seeing reality. If, in hindsight, you realize an issue that causes you problems should have been observed *before* problems started, ask for help. It's one of the reasons I recommend off-site sessions for serious deliberations. Make sure at least one capable Devil's Advocate attends these off-sites.

✦ **Lack of self-trust.** Many leaders struggle with seeing reality because they don't trust themselves. Throughout the Process, I recommend a number of books. For this situation, I highly recommend working through Malcolm Gladwell's *Blink*. It can help you recognize you do see a number of issues but don't trust yourself to believe what you see.

✦ **Divisive vision** (or "Visions Buy-in"). This may be the most important issue related to vision. Some people might not sign on if they know the vision doesn't suit them. That's a good thing. It's important for your success to ensure potential hires know your vision before they sign on. Be careful here, though, and note this vital lesson: *Just because you want something to be true doesn't make it true.* Making sure potential hires buy into your vision before you hire them can help you stay out of trouble. And staying out of trouble in the first place is much easier than trying to get out of trouble later.

I frequently come across someone who seems so sharp, I get excited about hiring the person onto our crew. But before I get too carried away, I have to first determine if s/he is a good fit for the crew. Does s/he share the vision?

Example: Developing KiVisions Vision and Mission Statements

To help you develop your organization's vision and mission statements, let's walk through the thought process used to start KiVisions. When building KiVisions, I set our direction toward "developing Great Leaders," but I needed to determine a purpose. What did I hope to accomplish through these Great Leaders?

Too many people establish their vision on a transactional basis and primarily focus on short-term activities as a matter of exchange. An example is, "If you perform *this* task, I'll give you *that* reward." My mentors helped me realize that what I do today has a potentially long-term, transformational effect. I came to realize *why* I was so intent on developing Great Leaders: to provide a cadre of those who would get our country On Course to a better tomorrow. Thus, the company's vision statement is intended to keep people focused in the moment while looking toward future outcomes.

Follow That Still, Small Voice

Many have asked me, "How do I know what my real purpose is?" I wish I had the universal answer. I can only tell you how I derived my purpose, which led me to establish the vision for my company. It comes from something I was taught as a child, which seemed bogus then, but it worked for me. Very simply, follow that still, small voice—the one you "hear" over and over.

Sure, there are still days when I wonder if I'm on the right course. But those days are overpowered by others that confirm I'm doing exactly what I was meant to do. *The key: Only you know what that still, small voice is saying, so listen!*

KiVisions Vision Statement

Develop Great Leaders *today* who keep us on course to a better *tomorrow*.

With our vision statement in hand, it was time to prepare our mission statement. Our Mission needed to be a direct outflow of our vision. What would we do to achieve our Vision? Our Mission Statement should help all current and potential stakeholders better understand what we are about. That's true for you, too.

The KiVisions Mission Statement

Help good people become Great Leaders so they can Unlock, Engage, and Optimize their potential and the potential of those they do or will lead.

You might choose, as we did, to develop additional guidelines, such as our Values, Axiom, Motto, and Standards of Excellence. At minimum, however, establish a Vision Statement and Mission Statement to ensure that you start On Course.

Consistency of Vision/Mission/Actions

Consistency can be a stumbling block. It might be tempting to take the easy way out using Poster Proxy Leadership. With this approach, you find several great posters that promote the kind of action, thinking, and behaviors you want your crew to adopt. The posters replace the need for you and the rest of the leadership team to model the same behavior, right? They sure come in handy as something you can point to when one of the "slugs" in your organization isn't acting the way you'd like!

That might sound cynical coming from quite a positive person. But I'm also realistic because I've run into a number of Wanna-Be and False Leaders in my day. My sardonic view of their leadership "strategy" is my way of asking you to avoid this style.

Know that becoming a Great Leader is a long road with few shortcuts. Poster Proxy Leadership aligns with the Left Hand, Right Hand warning mentioned earlier. Assuming that pretty posters of the company's Vision and Mission statements will induce the crew to instantly "buy in" and everything will turn out fine is left-hand thinking. If that's true, then what are the odds of success?

That said, wonderful companies such as Successories (founded by Mac Anderson) produce visual reminders in books and posters for you and the staff. Just don't use these as replacements for leading and modeling what you want from your crew.

Vision/Mission/Actions Exercise

To ensure your actions are consistent with your Vision and Mission, consider using what KiVisions uses to support individual and organizational development. The Vision/Mission/Actions Exercise is available in the On Course Pre-Flight Baseline that will help you take the steps necessary to prepare for "flight".

Both statements should serve as your means to articulate to others (and remind yourself) the future you desire to create and the part you will play. They should incorporate your *raison d'etre:* the reason you and your organization exist (if they're in alignment).

As we work through the series, we will explain why your *raison d'etre* is bigger than the job you go to each day. Your Vision and Mission, as articulated in your statements, should be an outflow of a deliberate process to accomplish something meaningful—for both you and those you serve. I recommend you make both statements simple and clear.

To make the outcome of your Vision and Mission Statements powerful, work through the Operational Focus Tool. It starts with determining the value you provide to your clients.

Your Value Proposition

The discussion that follows may sound off course, but bear with me. Although this exercise might help with your next car purchase, that's not the point of it. Instead, citing common events and activities can help clarify leadership topics.

When you bought your last car, what factors did you consider when making your decision? You probably started by looking at your needs: price, reliability, safety, legroom, the number of passengers, fuel economy, and more. Then you probably considered your desires: color, model, gull-wing doors, turbo-charged, gets from 0-60 mph quickly—you get the picture.

Buying a car, especially a new one, is usually a happy event. But did the last car you bought completely meet all your needs and desires? Not likely. Life offers more choices than ones that are realistic for most people. Does that mean all decisions should be based on practical needs? Not at all. Life would be boring if it didn't include a few things you desire.

So how do you choose the most important options? Consider these suggestions:

- ✦ Do your best to understand *why* the various factors you selected made the list.

- ✦ Discern the effect of those factors if they're included in the ultimate purchase.

- ✦ Don't allow any one factor to drive your decision.

- ✦ Because you probably can't meet all your needs and desires, choose those factors that will result in your best *value*.

Wise advice: *You can't be all things to all people.* You need to determine specific factors to concentrate on—ones that uniquely define you. They help you stand out and make it clear to your client or customer how choosing you is the best option.

Operational Focus Tool

Use KiVisions Operational Focus Tool to help you and your organization show your buyers why you offer the best value over your competitors.

Taken together, these factors are known as your Value Proposition.

Who Is Your Client or Customer?

I don't recommend you subscribe to the theory espoused

in the movie "Field of Dreams": *If you build it, they will come.* The question you need to answer is, "who am I/are we choosing to serve?" Before tackling the Operational Focus Tool, know your clients! A client or customer is anyone who might buy what you are selling. To define your primary buyers, you need to know their pulse points—what they need and want—so you can offer a good fit.

It's best to determine your Value Proposition before you open your doors—but you'd better do it eventually or you may be forced to close them! If you can, obtain input from a mastermind group you belong to or a good coach who specializes in this type of work. If you've been in business a while, include your crew in this exercise. People working in your company have lots of helpful insights.

Exercise to Determine Your Company's Value Proposition

Although this exercise can be performed at multiple levels, let's use a company as an example. Once you have an idea of the products and/or services you will offer, brainstorm a list of factors that explain *why* your products are preferable to similar products available on the market. As in the car-buying example, include how your products satisfy both their needs and desires.

Next, pare down the list to the most important differentiators for your organization. A few factors may stand out. You might want to combine certain factors into an inclusive term that easily identifies the concept. For example, in my

> role as hospital administrator, I had to ensure we provided valuable healthcare. Therefore, we focused on the primary factors of cost, quality, and access. Quality was a term that included many facets of healthcare.

The key: *Focus on only the most important factors.* Once you have your list, sleep on it. Rejoin the deliberation the next day to see if you missed factors or need to make modifications. Don't expect this process to take only two days, however. You'll likely revisit it periodically until you zero-in on exactly what differentiates you from your customers' other options.

Figure 5.1
The KiVisions Decision Triangle

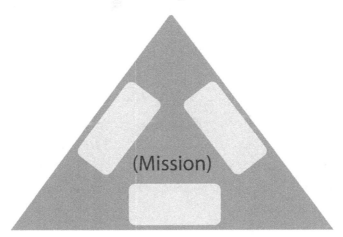

I suggest using the KiVisions Decision Triangle in Figure 5.1 to display your most important factors in both the discernment stage and the use stage. It gives you a visual representation that you and others can debate about—and decide upon—the most important factors for achieving your vision, mission, and goals. Plus, this Operational Focus Process points you in the right direction for getting buy-in from your stakeholders.

To stay focused on what you want to accomplish, place your Mission Statement in the center of the Triangle. (Abbreviate if you must; for example, we display "HGPBGL" in our Triangle where we would normally offer our "quick" mission as Help Good People Become Great Leaders.) Then pare down your choices to the three most important factors that will drive your operational focus.

Customer Pulse Points

Now that you have a basic idea of the Process, let's go into key areas. As you choose the primary customers you intend to serve, use their pulse points to help you decide the factors you will focus on more than others. By understanding their needs and desires, you will be better able to position yourself as their desired option.

For example, big box stores are competing mostly on price so the cost of the items they sell is essential, but they also need to have some measure of quality built into their products. (Often higher prices equal higher quality, but most of us realize that correlation doesn't always exist.) Plus in DIY (Do-It-Yourself) stores, the novice homeowner could use good advice on how to tackle a problem or a project. In such cases, service would be high on the list of factors. Location, which is critical to many operations, is less significant for these DIY stores but still important.

On the other end of the spectrum, many Ferrari customers focus on price but from a totally different perspective. They like the distinction provided by a highly expensive car that few can afford.

Plus, they also want high quality and performance. So the companies selling to these elite customers will have an altogether different set of focal points to balance.

Consider this printing business commercial: "Our competitor will give you any two of these: cheap, fast, or good." If you're in the printing business, can you meet your customers' needs with only two of the top three? Let's say your company focuses on fast and good. You might provide the best option for a customer who's in a bind and needs a job completed quickly. But ask, will this approach work as an overall strategy? Most printing customers include cost as one of their primary factors in choosing a service. It's not likely enough customers will be willing to pay a high cost for last-minute service steadily—especially when they have other options. The trick is to ensure you can deliver all three well.

Finding the Sweet Spot

To help your clients or customers understand why you are their best choice, determine how much focus should be placed on each factor. Like the recipes of a world-class chef, proportions are important: Too much focus on one item will not produce the best result. To determine your Value Proposition requires finding the sweet spot within that mix of factors you chose.

Do this: Figuratively draw an arc from the center of each factor toward the middle of the triangle. To indicate greater weight, the radius of the most important factors will be longer than less important factors. The sweet spot—that area where you provide greatest value—will be somewhere at the intersection of these arcs, the place that correctly balances the factors. Although some factors may have more priority than others, make sure you don't concentrate too much on any one factor. See Figure 5.2.

Figure 5.2
The KiVisions Decision Triangle Showing Sweet Spot

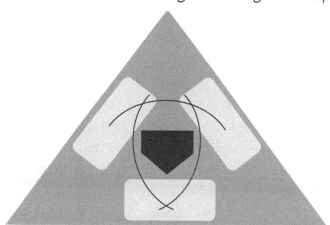

You would ask, "Can two or more companies have the same factors?" Yes, they can. If they serve a similar market, they will likely be direct competitors and their products/services might be classified as commodities. This limits differentiation.

The next logical question is, "How can you come out on top when you have the same factors as your competitor(s)?" In this case, it will come down to how well you execute the factors you list as being your Value Proposition. (Future books in this series will address execution in detail.)

You would then ask, "Value for *whom?*" You have to consider the key stakeholders, and you can use a Decision Triangle to determine who these people are.

Healthcare Example

In the case of our medical center, we knew our key stakeholders had to be integrally involved. For example, it's much easier to provide the best possible care to patients if members of the Medical Center staff feel as if they're part of the process—that is, they feel they have a degree of ownership. As with most things, unlocking the potential of staff members not only improves productivity, but their knowledge, experience, and insight ensure the organization is heading in the right direction.

As medical centers do, we had hundreds of possible focus areas but carefully considered the constraints over which we had varying levels of control such as resources (e.g., capital, qualifications of the staff, etc.). Some factors conflicted with others (e.g., high quality and low price). The solution to this dilemma is up to the leaders.

It became clear we had to focus on factors that would maintain the best possible care, was accessible to our patient population, and did so at the lowest possible cost. Notice I didn't say price. For those in industries with similar issues, let's clarify this.

Healthcare is a bit of an anomaly in the business world because most would say the "customer" implies whoever is paying. However, I met thousands of patients each year as I made my rounds throughout the facilities for which I was responsible, and I rarely met the primary payor. In our case, that payor was an insurance organization: government, private, or other. That meant our patients weren't interested in the price because someone else was paying their bill. (It was amazing to hear a small cadre of patients complain about a $25 co-pay for a procedure or hospital stay that actually cost thousands of dollars.)

Our payors paid us a set rate per procedure based on an algorithm. To remain viable, our administration team had to focus on costs. Hopefully, your situation is much cleaner and you can focus on price more than cost.

The next question would be "Why three items?" Three is a lower limit. Although I've worked with many people who have a laundry list they're struggling to manage, it's just as common for clients to believe they should focus on only one factor. That, too, is a mistake. The upper limit is five factors. Any more than five dilutes the efforts of the organization.

KiVisions Value Proposition

At KiVisions, our Value Proposition was derived as a result of measured steps. To achieve the greatest value for our customers, we Help Good People Become Great Leaders (our mission) because we do the following:

#1: Unlock, Engage, and Optimize human potential. Our competitors tout their ability to help people unlock their potential, but we go further. Compare this to a door. Why unlock it if you're not going to step through? That's why we also help engage and optimize that potential after it's unlocked. We do this through our innovative KiVisions Leader Development Process that offers the Successful Ventures in Human Dynamics Model, the Gyroscope System, and the Challenge to Leaders. As discussed, our process succeeds because it's geared to helping leaders at their expected level of leader readiness.

#2: Provide our clients numerous options relative to their willingness and ability to engage. Earlier, I claimed our country's main problem is that it's disengaged from what's vital to its future success. Plus, I've asked you to help with the reengagement process. KiVisions provides a myriad of options that include but aren't limited to the following:

✦ Three brands to meet various needs:

+ Soaring Leaders Academy™ (our teaching/mentoring brand)

+ True Leaders Forum™ (our coaching brand)

+ Impact on Results™ (our consulting brand)

✦ The opportunity to have a Wingman who will "watch your 6."

Watch Your 6 O'Clock

As you make progress and Grow Forward, it helps to have somebody looking out for your best interests. Think of the face of a clock in which 12 o'clock represents what's directly in front of you and 6 o'clock represents what's often the most difficult thing to see—what's directly behind you.

✦ The best delivery methods include the effort to continually explore what we believe and adapt it. (For example, online options are available in addition to our face-to-face options.) Plus, we're always looking for additional ways to engage with good people who want to become Great Leaders.

#3: Getting many people back On Course requires a RAVOlUtion. Not a violent revolution but a peaceful RAVOlUtion (explained in Chapter 9: The Foundation for Success.)

Figure 5.3 provides an example of the desired outcome of this process. When accomplished with diligence, it will serve multiple functions. Its primary purpose is to provide a visual representation that focuses your staff in ways that help your organization become a leader in your space.

Figure 5.3
KiVisions Decision Triangle Showing Desired Outcomes

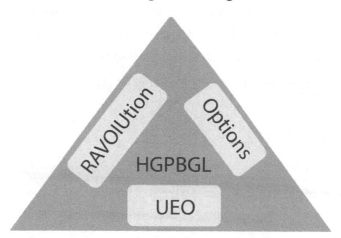

Use this tool to help you produce your own Value Proposition and introduce it to your clients and customers.

Discerning Your Personal Value Proposition

You might be asking, "Can I use the Operational Focus Tool to determine my personal Value Proposition?" The answer is "absolutely." The KiVisions Decision Triangle can assist here as well by changing the title from *Operational to Personal* Focus Tool. Look for a similar result for you or your organization.

Have You MAPD Out Your Life?

The Operational Focus Tool helps you sell others on what your organization offers. By comparison, the Personal Focus Tool helps you clarify your priorities on the path that leads to a fulfilling life. This

process can be more difficult for individuals than the one for organizations because establishing focal points for a product or service
is less personal and thus less emotional. As for an organization, to
determine your personal Value Proposition, discern the factors that
will best help you derive success and satisfaction.

The recommended process is a series of Right Questions.

Right Question #1

"What do you want to do with your life?"

You might call this your Strategic Direction or Purpose. Frequently, people respond with "to make a difference—a positive difference."

One of my mentors helped me realize I was best served by first
having a big-picture sense of what I wanted to do. At the time, I was
focused on an immediate issue, a micro perspective. Over the years,
I realized how valuable this macro perspective can be. It helped me
identify the number-one factor to concentrate on when ascertaining
my vision and my personal Value Proposition. That's *my purpose*. Doing so not only provided direction, it helped me feel more confident
that I was **M**aking **a P**ositive **D**ifference. As a result, I'm living a
more fulfilling life.

Today, my two broad ideas from a macro perspective are: 1) take
good care of those closest to me, and 2) make my life count by leaving this world better than I found it.

Having said that, I wish I could tell you my life has been a
straight shot from where I was to where I wanted to be. Does this
chart in Figure 5.4 reflect the path you've trodden? It provides a
picture of mine.

Figure 5.4

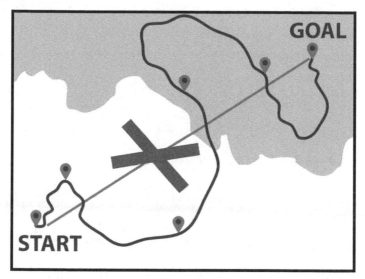

With so many opportunities and options available, it's easy to drift. How do you keep "drifting" from becoming a problem? *By resolving your purpose.*

Lots of people get hung up on this and want to be perfect from the start, but that's not likely. To follow Cal Newport's advice in his book *So Good They Can't Ignore You* (see Appendix D), set your macro purpose first. Then keep working to discern what you are called to be and do today.

Making **a P**ositive **D**ifference speaks to the kind of person you are and want to be. Keep this in mind as you narrow your options to a micro perspective. Hopefully, you'll find your ultimate calling, even if it takes a while and includes a few wrong turns. As you search for what you "should" be doing in the short term, don't get hung up on the micro perspective. It can change many times based on situations, circumstances, and your introspections.

For each position in my adult life, I had to consider a multitude of things before I could discern how best to proceed in my diverse background of experiences: flying, running medical centers, teaching college students, and now Helping Good People Become Great Leaders.

Right Question #2

"How best can I accomplish my purpose?"

Explore this question by looking at your *potential;* start by discerning your special talents. You could explore any number of tools including Dr. Clifton's *Strengths Finder,* on which Tom Rath's book *StrengthsFinder 2.0* is based. (See Appendix D.)

You may have heard someone say, "You can do *anything* as long as you put your mind to it." One of my tangential mentors, John Maxwell, would dispute that claim. As part of the *Maxwell Plan for Personal Growth,* John Maxwell has a segment titled "Determine the areas of your life in which you need to grow." He wrote:

> Watching people grow, I've discovered that, on a scale of 1 to 10, people can only improve about two notches. For instance, I love to sing; that's the good news. The bad news is that I can't carry a tune. . . . Now, let's be generous and say that, as a singer, I'm a 'two.' If I put lots of money, effort, and energy into developing my voice, perhaps I can grow into a 'four.' Newsflash: on a 10-point scale, four is still below average. With regards to my career, it would be foolish for me to focus my personal growth on my singing voice. At best I'd only become an average singer, and no one pays for average. Don't work on your weaknesses. Devote yourself to fine tuning your strengths.[10]

By asking yourself this question—"How best can I accomplish my purpose?"—you can get to your core question: "Of all the skills I have, what combination will help me live with confidence, energy, and enthusiasm?"

Get to Your Core

Skill A + Skill B + Skill C =
Confidence/Energy/Enthusiasm

When I was teaching undergraduates at the Smeal College of Business at Penn State University, I had multiple "customers." One group the college attempted to make strong connections with included those planning to hire our students at some point. Many corporate recruiters told me that students from the Smeal College of Business have incredible technical skills compared with recruits from other schools. But as they offered, like most of the students they recruit, their soft skills could use improvement. Soft skills include the ability to communicate, be a team player, adapt to circumstances, solve problems, observe situations critically, and so on.

In evaluating the skills that bring you confidence, energy, and enthusiasm, don't leave out your soft skills. They seem to be in short supply and thus in great demand.

Right Question #3

"Should I _____?"

Fill-in-the-blank with whatever you're thinking about doing. "Should I" means "would it be a good thing for me to . . .?" This leads to a third factor to explore: principles. Looking at principles means considering issues from the legal (issues of law), ethical (societal norms), and moral (personal values) perspectives. Think of your principles like this: *What will you always do and what will you never do, even if threatened?*

We've seen violence, but most workplace threats people face are more likely to be financial than physical. Too many people whose livelihood is threatened make bad decisions, often due to not asking themselves what they should *always* or *never* do. Once they know the answer, they commit to it. *Your* answers require you to prepare accordingly.

Determining Your Principles

You are in the best position to determine the right factors for you. If you sought help for discerning something this important, you'd be displaying strength, not weakness.

Please share what you resolved with this exercise. When you do, you'll receive credit and possible inclusion of your "best practices" on the KiVisions Facebook page. Send a note to KiVisions@KiVisions.com.

Connection with ACE

Some have asked, "Is there a connection between the factors for determining my personal Value Proposition and the ACE mantra (that is, Live with an **A**bundance Mentality, **C**oncentrate on Priorities, and **E**arnestly Pursue Your Purpose . . . with Passion!)?" Yes, there is.

Key Words from the Mantra	Connects With
Abundance	Principles
Concentrate on Priorities	Potential
Earnestly Pursue Your Purpose	Purpose

Leaders are role models. We need leaders to help this country get On Course to achieve greater Peace, Freedom, and Prosperity by modeling the tenets of ACE—and living them every day.

It's up to you and/or your organization to achieve your Value Proposition. Which factors will you focus on? As noted, you can use the Operational Focus Tool to point you in the desired direction and get buy-in from your stakeholders. Plus, this tool can be used for every level in the organization.

Chapter 6 addresses how you can make each aspect of the Value Proposition a reality to give you the best chance of achieving your Vision.

ACHIEVING THE VISION—7 STEPS

W hat is the best way to make good decisions today that will still be good decisions tomorrow (that is, to achieve the Vision you established)? Follow the template provided in this chapter. It involves these seven steps to properly outfit the "plane":

1. Establish a mission plan.

2. Press-to-test your plan.

3. Execute the plan.

4. Measure progress periodically.

5. Reflect on what you learned.

6. Take necessary action.

7. Revisit steps 1-6 repeatedly.

Let's look at each step in detail

Step 1. Establish a Mission Plan.

First, determine the steps you'll take to achieve your Vision. What differentiates this planning process from others? It concentrates on bringing your Value Proposition into reality. (The steps that follow are modifications of my planning strategic missions in the Air Force.)

Mission planning has been around for many years. Even so, some doubt its value. As Helmuth Von Moltke, Chief of Staff of the Prussian Army (1858-1888), stated, "No operation extends with any certainty beyond the first encounter with the main body of the enemy."[11] The shortened version reads, "No plan survives first contact." So what's the use of having a plan?

Consider the wisdom of General/President Dwight D. Eisenhower, the commander responsible for the operations that ultimately defeated Nazi Germany. He said, "I've always found that plans are useless *but planning is indispensable*"[12] (my italics). Ike was smart enough to understand that *planning* allows flexibility by exploring *why* we're doing what we're doing. It provides an in-depth look at how to bring about what we desire and the likely obstacles in our path. Planning gives us the ability to respond to situations we may encounter when we put the plan into effect.

As an anonymous quotation states: "Don't let your desire for victory override the need to develop the process that will lead to victory." That means the chance you'll achieve victory without a well-defined plan is slim.

A Necessary Step

The opportunity to fly is wonderful, but flyers don't relish some phases. Pre-Flight is one of them. During this phase, they have to examine the state of the aircraft. This is tedious and can be boring, especially because a defect is rarely discovered. As such, flyers might skip or cursorily perform the examination—not a wise move according to Dave Matheny who wrote about it in Sport Aviation magazine.[13]

Akin to pre-flight exams, mission planning is a necessary step to help you achieve the vision and avoid a crash.

Achieving the best results from our planning requires us to *commit* to first-class outcomes. Some people ask, "Are you sure we should commit to that? What if something comes up that causes us to settle for something less than first-class?" But why settle for less than the best possible outcome?

Questioners are often asked to explain how they derived their vision. Many have multiple visions and want to focus on the one that appears it will work out best. Then they list their successes to date and the measurements used to deem each a success. Typically, a hodge-podge of responses comes in with few meaningful victories among them.

Sure, you need to consider reality, but setting slightly unreasonable expectations might get you to realize the potential you have locked inside. Don't settle for what's unfulfilling! Find your focal point and maintain your commitment, even if the goal feels audacious.

Under-Promise and Over-Deliver?

I never agreed with this idea. Why should I buy what you're selling if you're promising to deliver something less than I want?

Instead, develop an excellent Value Proposition, cultivate excited clients, and make sure you meet or exceed the value you promise. Setting low expectations often yields low results, which is likely to set a mental attitude that you aren't capable of achieving more. This idea is especially important if you lead a crew of people because they will look to you as a role model. If they see you settling, they assume that mindset is expected. They'll either comply (not good) or look for another job with a better leader (also, not good).

First-Class Outcomes for Whom?

Think carefully about how much of the "whom" includes your ego. Too many leaders work to gain credit for themselves instead of their entire crew. Your inclinations might help you determine your current leader category. If your ego is driving the desired outcomes you're proposing, you might be the Wanna-Be Leader or, in the worst case, the False Leader. True Leaders aim for outcomes that reward the entire crew.

Commitment or Expediency?

Which is your modus operandi: commitment or expediency? One reason the Wright Brothers are admired is they committed to their task and proved the viability of the American Dream. Commitment is a form of integrity.

Too many people believe the American Dream is based on wealth accumulation. Let's rekindle the idea that every U.S. citizen has an equal opportunity to use his/her time and talents to achieve success *as each person measures it*. Let your hard work, determination, and initiative achieve your dream, not only financial prosperity.

Commitment List

Do you have a list of commitments and a clear understanding of what commitments you've made to whom and by when? If not, begin your list now. Review it periodically and see what, if anything, changes over time.

Make sure it's built on life balance. Please don't assume that to Unlock, Engage, and Optimize your potential you must be working 24/7 on what you might call your job. Instead, incorporate a clear look at all the priorities in your life. Balance the effort you place on each. Sure, your profession will likely be on this list, but to live a completely fulfilling life, include all your priorities. Only you can determine what those are.

But how fast should you travel? How far should you go? How high should you climb?

At this early stage, pick something that's relatively easy such as creating and monitoring your commitment list. Are your current commitments focused on priorities you established? Do you tend to over or under commit?

Next, give yourself a goal of committing to only those things that are true priorities for you over the next month. Complete the commitment(s) to the best of your ability. After a month, analyze your activities (relative to your commitments) and see what you've learned. If you need more work, make it happen. If you are somewhat successful, improve in this area. If you have significant success, then find the next item to target.

You are likely to discover that making improvements with your commitments helps you find the next item to work on.

Envision Your Success

Visualize your success. Use metrics or whatever you need to develop a crystal clear idea of what you're aiming for. Why? So you can recognize when you've achieved it. This visioning technique might also help you realize you've reached a place you didn't want to go. If you arrive at one of these points, don't assume you've failed. Au contraire. It's possible your efforts have taken you somewhere unexpected but quite positive. Envisioning success is one way to stay on track from beginning to end.

Post-it® Notes

How many Post-it® Notes have you used? I use a bunch! Did you know there was never a plan to invent this product?

In 1968, Spencer Silver was working at 3M trying to create super-strong adhesives in building planes for the aerospace industry. Instead of that, he accidentally created an incredibly weak, pressure-sensitive adhesive agent. This adhesive didn't interest 3M decision makers who saw it as too weak to be useful. Its two basic features—first, when stuck to a surface, the paper can be peeled away without leaving residue and, second, the adhesive can be reused—weren't recognized as useful until 1977. That's when Post-it® Notes were invented.[14]

Don't assume all outcomes have potential success buried within. I'm merely suggesting you don't declare failure immediately if it appears you haven't reached your intended destination. See if you can discern value from the resources you have expended before you correct your course.

Determine Answers to the Right Questions

Well-considered answers to the Right Questions help you derive a plan for achieving the best outcomes. Caution: Don't make the mistake of jumping to "How do I/we __ (fill in the blank)" questions because other questions take priority.

The Right Questions will differ depending on whether you're planning for an individual, group, team, or organization. Plus, expectations will differ based on where you are on your journey. If you're an Emerging Leader, for example, you'll be at a significantly different point in your career than a Leader of Leaders.

Use these Right Questions to ask yourself about your personal progress:

+ Have my decisions been oriented toward only me, a few others and me, many others and me, or _____? (Take a realistic look at the effects of your past decisions.)

+ Have the outcomes of my decisions resulted in a track record of good, lasting results—or not? (Consider both what you've done and what you haven't done.)

+ Have I set high goals and achieved them? (Don't let yourself get blinded by your good decisions and outcomes, of which you likely have many. Also include those decisions that *didn't* result in your desired outcomes.)

+ Am I where I want to be?

+ Am I using my unique talents to the best of my ability?

+ Am I receiving the support I need? (By the same token, explore whether or not you're supporting the needs of others, which indicates an Abundance Mentality.)

✦ Am I on track to reach my five, ten, twenty-year goals? (This assumes you've determined goals for each of these milestones.)

✦ What makes me believe I'll be fulfilled when I reach those targets?

When you're comfortable with your answers to these questions, ask, "How do I get closer to where I want to be?"

Next, ask these Right Questions for your organization:

✦ Where are we currently? Consider these primary options:

+ *On Course:* the desired option—due to actions you are taking.

+ *Drifting:* You could be close to being On Course but if you're drifting, it will be by coincidence, not design or diligent effort to stay On Course.

+ *Off Course:* Often caused by Wanna-Be Leaders, this occurs when you've drifted so long, your path no longer resembles any intent you established when you started.

+ *Wrong Course:* Often caused by False Leaders who establish a vision that serves only him- or herself, the rest of the organization suffers from moving in a direction that's not conducive to achieving reasonable goals.

+ *Headed South:* In case you're unfamiliar with this euphemism, it has nothing to do with a compass reading. As the *Free Dictionary* (www.thefreedictionary.com) offers: "Headed South is to cease working or functioning; to quit, fail, or fall apart."

If your organization is deemed to be Headed South, you're in real trouble and may be about to crash and burn. Wanna-Be and False Leaders are typically in charge of organizations Headed South.

Possible Source of Confusion

A source of confusion might be in the "instruments" you are using to determine your heading. See the Heading Indicator in this chapter.

✦ How did we get here? (Make sure your discussion includes the good, the bad, and the ugly—for example, bad assumptions, bad direction to start, and more. Finger-pointing often starts here. As the leader, it's your job to ensure this doesn't turn into a blame fest instead of a sincere opportunity to help the organization improve.)

✦ Are we focused on the right things? (If not, revisit the Vision Test.)

✦ Are the risks you're taking worth the potential reward? (At the other end of the scale, make sure you aren't playing it too safe. Both of these extremes can indicate unhealthy, unbalanced organizations.)

✦ What's the next great challenge to tackle? (Good leaders always look to the future. Warning: Don't use looking forward as an excuse to dismiss the need to correct current problems. If you don't solve them now, you likely won't solve them in the future.) Don't forget to ask: What's the likely outcome if we do/don't accept this challenge?

When you're comfortable with the answers to the previous questions, it's okay to ask: How do we get closer to where we want to be?

Even though questions can spark discussion, they are ultimately useless until you derive your best answers. Be sure to do the following along the way.

Assess Risks/Rewards

Explore available options and assess the risks and/or rewards of doing (or not doing) each option. Don't confuse this assessment of risk with assessment of future risks/rewards, which are separate steps. When measuring risks, know that financial cost is only one factor; you need to measure cost in more than just dollars.

Case Study – Tylenol Scare vs. Ford Pinto

This case study compares the total cost to Johnson and Johnson of the 1982 Tylenol scare with that incurred by Ford regarding issues with the Pinto beginning in 1972.

The total costs for the two were significantly different as a result of how each company weighed current costs to long-term costs. Comparing how each company handled these issues, J&J won by considering the potential long-term costs. Its leaders were open about the problem, recalled the potentially tainted Tylenol products, and explained the new steps for safety they implemented.

Unfortunately, Ford attempted to hide the Pinto problems from current and prospective customers. It proved a valuable lesson; Ford has been more public about its issues since.

Is Your Plan Feasible?

Consider what makes you believe any of the options will achieve the vision. A lot of smart people have spent countless amounts of time, energy, and resources attempting to achieve their visions.

Great things can happen when entrepreneurs put their money or the money they secure from investors at risk. These investors consider the risks and potential rewards with serious deliberation because they have skin in the game. When public money is "gambled" in this fashion it feels uncomfortable because the same motivations are not in place.

Because I highlighted the problems with our entertainment society earlier, let me offer an example that extends the entertainment problem to our state governments. The issue: Taxpayer dollars being used to support movies, sport stadiums, and so on. These public-private investments are intended to yield a positive return for the communities entering into these agreements. Research shows the return leans toward being negative. For example, a 2009 report[15] from my home state, Pennsylvania, identified that the film tax credit has a negative effect on the state treasury. (To be fair, the report reveals that including all ancillary activity, there's a net positive effect, but I found it difficult to validate the ancillary effect.)

This appears to be consistent with other programs around the country. So why do we continue to put tax payer money at risk for these questionable programs?

Are Your Parameters Reasonable?

Explore the likelihood the option chosen will achieve the vision *within reasonable parameters.* Many organizations skip or gloss over this step, wanting to believe they have the magic answer to all problems.

Instead, they need to get real. They're human. If they don't fix it now, they're likely to go "down the rabbit hole" too deeply. Often, it's only when people/organizations hit bottom that they finally resolve to fix problems. Many act this way because they hate to fail. The search for success can become an addiction—like the gambler who knows the next bet will bring victory . . . or the one after that.

When things aren't going according to plan, good advice would be to set parameters and give them an entire relook before you throw more good money after bad.

Do You Have the Necessary Resources?

The next step is to ensure you have the necessary resources to accomplish the mission. For example, do you have the crew you need to make this happen? Will you require external support? Many organizations screw this up because they wildly assume the personnel necessary to fulfill the mission will be available. Too many would-be leaders generate great ideas without clearly identifying who will bring those ideas to fruition. Often, would-be leaders add duties to their current staff without ensuring there's a benefit to them (the staff people) for accepting those new responsibilities. This approach is not recommended.

Make sure you have the resources in place or available. That doesn't mean all those resources have to come from within the organization, but consider training and/or development needs for the people responsible for key areas of the plan.

How Will You Measure Progress?

As leader, it's your responsibility to ensure a system of measurement that uses the right instruments is in place. The better options also serve another goal of leaders: to effectively communicate expectations.

Too many leaders believe the subjective nature of soft skills doesn't allow for measuring progress. I beg to differ. You can (and need to!) measure progress in all essential facets of your organization.

Dashboard

You may be familiar with various tools used for measuring an organization's activities. Most common measurements fall within the province of the manager's role. A primary vehicle used to display the overall "health" of the organization is the Dashboard.

A typical dashboard is represented in the following graphic.

A Typical Dashboard

The advantage of using gauges and instruments (whether in business or flying) is their ability to provide a quick overview of your current status on important issues. They also help target those issues that have the greatest need for attention. What set of instruments for measuring status/progress is found within the leader's role? As you work through the series, you'll learn about a set of instruments that assist in your role as leader. They mirror aviation instruments that helped me many years ago. I know firsthand there's no mistaking one gauge for another. First is the Heading Indicator.

Heading Indicator

Start by using these instruments to measure your own performance. Later on in the series, more advanced reflections will help you measure the results of higher ups, direct reports, peers, customers, vendors, and other key stakeholders. These instruments keep everyone involved focused on *where they are* and *what they need to improve* to get where they want to go.

The aircraft outline in the center of the gauge is intentionally pointed North (N). For ease and standardization, North represents the direction that allows you and the organization to achieve your Vision—described as being On Course

Determining Tolerance

Caution: Instruments must be "calibrated."

First, determine how you'll measure your progress. Part of this requires a discussion about tolerance and knowing how tightly you will maintain your course.

The Principle of Tolerance

Although the application of tolerance is different in the U.S. Air Force than in business planning, the principle is the same. When flying high-altitude missions, we were authorized to be within five miles of our planned course. Five miles one side or the other at 35,000 feet over the 12,000-mile-wide Pacific Ocean is totally acceptable; there's lots of space and not much in the way.

However, many of our missions require we avoid being detected by enemy radar. In these segments, we'd fly "low level" (i.e., at or below 400 feet off the ground or ocean). Being five miles one side or the other of our planned course when we were zooming along at low level wasn't acceptable; it was perilous.

Why not have the same tolerances for all processes? After all, people aren't machines. My longest flights lasted more than thirty-six hours *in the air;* briefings, pre-flight, and post-flight activities are not included in that figure. Most of those missions were flown at high altitude where the wide tolerances were acceptable. No one would have survived thirty-six hours in the more intense experience of flying at 400 feet.

Stress can cause people to perform amazingly well but only in short bursts because stressful activity is also exhausting. Know your limits and the limits of the people working with and for you. Don't induce unnecessary stress. If you have an item to accomplish that's both urgent and important, tight tolerances might be the order of the day. For other issues, tolerances can be more relaxed. The goal is to make sure your tolerances are consistent with your needs. (We will address expectations and tolerances through much of the series.)

A question: Do you require that every communication within your organization be perfect? I don't. I recommend adopting a system that recognizes only documents that will be seen/used outside of the area of the organization for which you are responsible. Only these need the "perfection" standard.

As long as you make it clear which standards apply for the phase a document is in, then internal memos, drafts, and similar informal documents can be held to a lower standard *as long as the message is clear and accurate.* The savings in time and frustration can have a marked improvement on your overall productivity. Concentrating on priorities is a key aspect of a leader, so aim to set and reinforce reasonable standards.

Once you know how you'll measure your progress, next determine *how often* you will report on your progress. This is a matter of
best practice that will change based on many factors. Organizations
that are flying smoothly likely don't need to report as frequently as
those that have issues. If you're in an industry with many competitors, you can likely find a trove of data on best practices.

Dead Reckoning

Especially when I was in one of those flight modes that had high
tolerances, I used dead reckoning as a fairly quick and usually accurate form of navigation. Here's how it works in flight: From a known
starting point, I kept track of my heading, speed, and elapsed time to
calculate my likely current position.

You can apply a similar process in business. Even the SEC allows
publicly traded companies to use estimates on quarterly financial
statements. With all the responsibilities a leader has, estimating progress toward the vision can be a welcome relief. That said, until you
prove you're competent in leading others, I don't recommend dead
reckoning without confirming your progress through other means.

In fact, begin by testing yourself. Through experience, you can
gain the ability to assess the organization, the people in it, the changes in your market, and so on. As an example, True Leaders work
continually on their emotional intelligence. This helps them improve
their awareness of what's happening around them and accurately assess the situation. By using emotional intelligence, they might sense
that two key players are not working collaboratively or understand
that a communique you sent out requires enhancement. These "gut
instinct" moves will improve as you measure the impact of actions
you take.

Once you develop a fairly accurate awareness, you can add dead reckoning as a less sophisticated, less time-consuming tool to estimate your progress at appropriate points. Instead of always having to use scientific methods (e.g., capture actual data through extensive means) to confirm you are On Course, your ability to perceive the likelihood of being still headed in the right direction gives you time to focus on other leadership issues.

Adopting and becoming proficient with tools such as the Dashboard and Heading Indicator—as well as developing skills in determining tolerances and eventually dead reckoning—help leaders advance through the levels of leader readiness—that is, from Emerging Leader to Leader with History to Leader of Leaders.

Step 2. Press-to-Test Your Plan.

Once again, a flying analogy is relevant. Press-to-test comes from a lesson I learned early in my flying career. It may have saved my crew and me on more than one occasion.

Press-to-Test

The planes we flew in the Air Force had various gauges or sensors with a press-to-test button. If we doubted we were getting a correct reading from our instruments/gauges, we pressed the button to confirm they were in proper working order. We received either visual or auditory feedback if the gauge/instrument was working or no feedback if it wasn't. Receiving the response we expected indicated the information was likely reliable.

Start by getting impressions from key stakeholders as a test run. See what they think before you go live. You might find stumbling blocks you hadn't noticed previously. Plus, this allows you to gauge and build buy-in.

So why press-to-test your plan? First, because too many "leaders" expect the crew to blindly fall in line, which is *not* the way to Unlock, Engage, and Optimize human potential. Instead, help people follow your lead by ensuring they have a clear idea of the direction you intend to take the organization. Especially if you are embarking on a new venture or direction, do your best to help people understand where you plan to go and why. Let them provide feedback; are they with you on this endeavor or not.

I sometimes needed to perform a press-to-test in flight, but I always checked the gauges and instruments before takeoff. Likewise, if you cultivate an environment that allows people to ask questions and offer input, you'll likely reduce the number of "in-flight emergencies." Plus, key stakeholders may provide insight that helps you make better decisions.

Depending on the feedback you get, *modify the plan* as necessary. It's certainly easier to make changes before you take off than while you're "in the air." Interestingly, some people believe this step isn't necessary. That's when I ask them this question I learned from Coach Wooden of UCLA basketball fame: "If you don't have time to do it right, when will you find time to do it over?"

Step 3. Execute the Plan.

As important as this step is, once you get here, there isn't much to say about it. Now you need to play your role as outlined by the plan. (As you go through the series, it goes deeper into what Great Leaders do during all stages.) Let the people working with/for you do their jobs. Sure, no plan survives first contact; but when the leaders in the organization are trained and developed well, they can manage the issues that arise. It's best to release any concern about their ability to improvise, adapt, and overcome. People tend to meet high expectations.

Step 4. Periodically Measure Progress.

One of the best explanations of the need to measure progress comes from Andy Grove of Intel fame in his book *High Output Management:* "To illustrate an objective and a key result, consider the following: I want to go to the airport to catch a plane in an hour. That is my objective. I know that I must drive through towns A, B, and C in 10,

20, and 30 minutes respectively. If I've been driving for 20 minutes and haven't yet made town A, I know I'm lost. Unless I get off the highway and ask someone for directions, I probably won't make my flight."[16]

When you don't quite meet expectations, consider these possible reasons:

+ The Left Hand, Right Hand situation

+ The "fog and friction" conundrum: I have studied numerous military theorists in officer development. One of those was a long-winded bloke named Clausewitz who talked about fog and friction. To paraphrase his point: "Life is and always will be subject to uncertainty and the unexpected."

+ Internal sabotage: Unfortunately, leaders need to monitor the actions and designs of others. While direct competitors challenge your organization for market share, sadly, some people in the organization intentionally thwart the collective effort. As difficult as it may become, leaders are responsible for dealing with these issues.

Again, from a macro perspective, you need to determine if you're On Course, Drifting, Off Course, on the Wrong Course, or Headed South. Numerous tools are at your disposal. Many metrics depend on your type of organization, but certain tools work in most organizations. These include well-crafted surveys (both internal and external, as appropriate) and honest feedback from your crew and trusted advisors.

To start, however, limit your evaluation to self-reflection. Pick a time in your life when you set a personal goal and then worked to achieve that goal. Here are examples of self-reflections by leaders in each of our leader categories.

True Leaders would reflect that they did what was needed by the time it needed to be done. Whether they felt like it or not, they did it in ways consistent with their values, and they achieved their goals. Or as they were measuring their progress, they realized they had planned poorly or failed to recognize the effect of things beyond their control. So at these midpoints, they modified their course to ensure they achieved their goals. Or after working to achieve the goals for a time, they realized what it would take to achieve them was more costly than anticipated. They'd have to amend their plan and potentially change their goals. Or, due to a black swan event,[17] their original planning factors would have to be significantly, maybe totally, modified to include changing their goals.

Achieving the original goals in all facets would be the best case, but life doesn't always work that way—even for those who plan, prepare, and execute well. Because True Leaders operate from an ACE mindset, however, they find a way to eventually achieve their goals while remaining consistent with their values.

Wanna-Be Leaders *might* find that everything turned out in their favor and they achieved their original goals. It's not likely, but it's possible. A more probable scenario might indicate the Wanna-Be Leaders failed in the planning, preparation, and/or execution phases. They lacked either diligent effort or understanding of what was necessary to achieve the goal, so they didn't reach it. They damaged their reputation as a result. Or they realized at some midpoint they were Off Course. Being afraid to admit they were less than perfect, they continued along the path and blamed circumstances or other people for their lack of progress.

False Leaders might reflect they did what needed to be done by the time it needed to be done. That meant they were consistent with their values and achieved their original goal. The problem? A number of people were negatively impacted along the way. This is a natural outcome for them because False Leaders use people to get what they want. Their trustworthiness couldn't get lower. The False Leader and maybe some cronies are the only ones likely to have reaped any rewards.

If the leaders lived by the True Leaders Code, it's likely they lived up to the commitments made and ensured they did what was necessary to stay On Course. This would include spending on resources within set parameters, completing by the due date, and staying consistent with the organizational values. If so, the Heading Indicator can likely continue to point North.

Heading East. Wanna-Be Leaders likely got distracted or realized what it took to stay On Course was more than they could handle. To exacerbate the problem, most Wanna-Be leaders work for organizations that don't accept mistakes or help people grow from them. If you work for one of them, you're not likely to admit your mistakes nor seek the help you need. It's also improbable the organization will be headed North until this is corrected. If the situation is confirmed, the Heading Indicator would point East.

How far you are from where you *should be* will determine how far toward the East the aircraft outline would move.

Heading West. Did you agree to the vision of the organization but you've since worked at cross purposes for your own gain? As a False Leader, you're not likely to change the Heading Indicator on your own. Hopefully, your boss or, if you are the boss, a good board of directors monitors what's going on. Any of these people could display the Heading Indicator pointing West. Again, how far you *are* from where you *should be* will determine how far toward the West the aircraft outline would move.

Unfortunately, in my experience, too few boards take their governance duties seriously. It's easier to let things slide. For organizations in this situation, I say, "God help you."

Get the Help You Need

If this situation describes something close to what you're experiencing, please get the help you need. The people working with and for you desperately need you to get that help. If you work for a True Leader, as long as you admit your mistakes and do what it takes to become a True Leader, you'll be in the right flight path.

Step 5. Reflect and Decide on Necessary Action.

Did you learn you need to challenge your assumptions? Too many leaders miss this step, but it's vital for your own growth and that of your organization. What potentially outdated assumption should you challenge? Remember, *challenge* doesn't necessarily mean change. Challenge implies a mature approach to systems that might require updates.

Example of a Challenge

I'm a fan of zero-based budgeting[18] because of the need to conduct a review of all expenditures. Yes, it takes precious time, but it also requires a serious look at what has changed and what needs to be updated as a result.

What's Needed?

After you reflect on how your plan is working, your most likely options are Course Adjustments or Course Corrections.

✦ *Course Adjustments:* Minor issues will require an adjustment so you can continue toward your Vision. The Successful Ventures in Human Dynamics Model will help you determine how to deal with issues over which you have a measure of control as well as others over which you have little control or influence. Issues beyond your control/influence include those you need to avoid and others you need to address (with a few noted later in this chapter).

✦ *Course Corrections:* Major issues need to be addressed competently and quickly or the results could be devastating. These issues can result in crises when not dealt with appropriately. Making necessary Course Corrections often disrupts operations, but it's far worse to continue on the present course. Be cognizant of the cost that these corrective actions will incur (involving more factors than just dollars and time), but consider that the alternative might be totally unacceptable.

Corrective Aviation Maneuver

Drastic corrections can happen in aviation as well as in business—and the results can be life-saving. During a trip my friend took, he wondered about a frightening maneuver the pilots made during the landing approach of the plane in which he was a passenger. The only logical explanation was an unexpected obstacle (in the air or on the ground) that required radical action to avoid collision. The sudden movement frightened most of the passengers, and the captain offered no explanation. But if those pilots hadn't taken the corrective action, my friend might not be here today. An extreme example? Maybe, but it makes the point.

Specific situations require exploring all the factors before giving definitive advice on how to proceed. Consider this:

+ If things are bad, a total *revamp* might be required, and it might be advisable to start the Visioning process all over. If it gets to that point, be sure to do things right the next time.

+ Doing *nothing* is always an option and often a viable one. Some people promote the belief "If it ain't broke, don't fix it." This can be an excuse to avoid the pain and effort of making improvements. But still, don't assume giving a response is necessary to every situation. Timing can be critical, and it often takes a while for corrective actions to kick in.

Example of Over-Correction

My primary role in the B-52 was as navigator and bombardier (what we called radar navigators), but I took every opportunity to practice my piloting skills. My first time flying the B-52 at altitude, our pilot told me to climb. I pulled back on the yoke. When there was no immediate response (as I was used to in smaller aircraft), I pulled back more. When the airplane responded, I found out just how quickly a B-52 could climb.

Then I overcorrected in the descent. It was like trying to control a very big roller coaster. Later, I learned our pilot had turned off the transponder. So when Denver Center asked for our altitude, our pilot graciously responded "around Flight Level 350" (35,000 feet). In reality, we were above and below that level a couple times. It had taken time for my initial action to kick in, and that was magnified by my subsequent action. I was careful not to make that mistake again.

Give your corrections time to work if you can. This helps you grow as a leader and learn to trust your judgment, or what some call gut instinct.

Then based on your findings from Steps 4 and 5, take the next step.

Step 6. Take Necessary Action.

Why do people often need catastrophic events before they make course corrections? Examples from history: In feudal Japan, warlords fought each other brutally until an external threat to the nation arose. Only then did they cooperate. And isn't it funny, in a strange way, that what didn't seem possible before this threat became possible because of the threat.[19]

Many "leaders" use the "this time it's different" excuse as a way of not dealing with serious issues. Many are flummoxed and can't see the reasons for major problems. Because these excuses were prevalent immediately after the 2008 housing crisis, I wrote a series of articles starting with the phrase "I Refuse to Believe This Time It's Different"—because it rarely is. This series refuted those who believed the housing crisis would change our economic landscape forever. I refused to believe their postulation that we must modify our expectations, including no longer believing all who wanted a job would be able to have one.

The ability to contribute to the best of our ability is a prime aspect of living a fulfilled life. So I used the series as an opportunity to officially roll out the ACE idea. Although the economy hasn't recovered completely, I believe it will and even surpass old benchmarks.

Which is better: leaders who *solve* crises or those who *prevent* crises? The answer is obvious. Many speak about the need for leaders to exhibit commitment and integrity. If these are hallmarks of leaders, why do so few "leaders" *prevent* crises? In fairness, even the best plans and leaders can't prevent all crises. No crystal balls are handed out in leadership school.

Even a man as brilliant as Ben Bernanke, U.S. Federal Reserve Bank Chairman from 2006 to 2015, missed seeing the impending housing crisis that hit in 2008. In February 2007, he was quoted as saying: "Our assessment is that there's not much indication at this point that subprime mortgage issues have spread into the broader mortgage market, which still seems to be healthy. And the lending side of that still seems to be healthy."[20] The housing crisis started well before we felt the effects in 2008. Many missed it—even the top economist at the Fed. Had the "adults in the room" done something earlier, the carnage could have been lessened or perhaps even averted.

Why do many of the course corrections made as a result of catastrophic events put us *more* Off Course than if we'd done nothing?

Because in the midst of crises, panic and fear rule. Many succumb to the snake oil pressed on us by those with a scarcity mentality. They appear to be throwing us a life preserver, but it turns out to be an anchor.

Do *not* give in to fear. If you follow the process prescribed here, it's unlikely you'll have to respond to many emergencies you didn't foresee. Those that do come about will probably be caused by issues external to your operations.

Step 7. Revisit Steps 1-6 Repeatedly.

If you reach a point of No Joy, get the help you need.

chapter seven

BALANCING FORCES IN THE SUCCESSFUL VENTURES IN HUMAN DYNAMICS MODEL

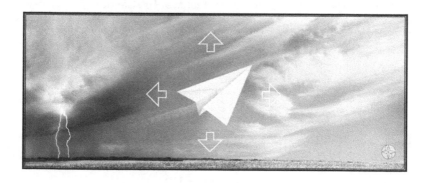

I n the Successful Ventures in Human Dynamics Model, 1) point the "plane" toward the desired destination, 2) properly outfit the "plane," and 3) balance the four forces to maintain "altitude/airspeed." When you do this, you'll be close to Earning Your Wings, the first rating that challenges True Leaders.

As discussed, similar to an aircraft, leaders must realize that the forces affecting their organization are interconnected—that is, a change in one affects the others. Carefully working through the Model ensures you're making decisions that will increase your chances of success.

As a reminder, no force is necessarily positive, no force is necessarily negative, but no matter what, they must be in balance. This is why proper instrumentation is important. (This will be addressed one instrument at a time to allow you to build a comfort level with each one going forward.) How can you use the Model to point your organization in the desired direction, get off the ground, and stay aloft?

Think of a leadership situation, positive or negative, that you're currently experiencing, have experienced, or have addressed as a case study. By exploring that situation in detail, determine the variables that made it a positive or negative experience using this Model. Further exploration helps you achieve greater success in future forays. (An example will follow after each aspect of the Model is explained.)

So far, we've worked to point the "plane" toward the desired destination (Vision) and ensure it is properly outfitted to accomplish the Mission and achieve the Vision. Now let's address the forces that help you "maintain altitude and airspeed."

Lift and Thrust: The Forces Necessary to Get Off the Ground and Climb

Lift

Think of Lift as how you get off the ground. Two possibilities: the first option, a lighter-than-air craft, is like a hot air balloon. (The problem is the only measure of directional control, more like influence, is up and down.) The second option, a heavier-than-air craft, is akin to your organization in which Lift is considered *potential* until Thrust is applied.

You might ask, "Why would you leave the safety of the ground?" Anyone who thinks ground travel is inherently safer than air travel is highly mistaken. Aircraft accidents make the news for two reasons: 1) The carnage is typically greater than in most roadway accidents, and 2) The number of accidents with human injury in aircraft versus ground transportation is small by almost any measure.

If you've lost a friend or loved one in an aircraft or land-based vehicular accident, I'm sorry. I know the pain caused by both. We take risks in life, but I submit that air travel is a relatively safe venture. A colleague in the leader development business uses bus travel as his analogy for moving an organization forward. But other than Rosa Parks' defiance, name something that happened on a bus and changed how the world works! Most people would rather travel in a sleek aircraft.

Besides the fact that air travel is statistically safer than ground travel, flying offers two distinct advantages. First, you're able to take a more direct path to your destination as opposed to dealing with obstacles on the ground and navigating on preset roadways. Second, as the old saying goes, most people have a need for speed and can reach their destination more quickly by air.

To connect these ideas to leadership, think about what *lifts* people's spirits, including:

+ a deeply inspiring belief that you have something positive to contribute

+ an opportunity to use your knowledge and skills

+ a sense of achievement

+ a feeling of connectedness to a crew of workers

+ a knowingness that "we" made a positive difference

+ a belief that the people you work for and with care

+ a possibility of rewards and recognition for doing a good job

+ an environment that fosters trust

+ a habit of effective communication

+ a meaningful training and development effort

This list represents what people in authority should promote in their organizations. However, they're usually only cultivated routinely under a True Leader.

Another good thing about Lift: The higher we get, the less Thrust is needed to move forward. All the forces involve at least one caveat, and for Lift, it's these: The higher you go, the greater mastery is required and the more equipment is needed. Plus, you could get too high and lose perspective, and if you climb too quickly, you could stall.

Have you ever been in an organization that stalled? Then you've seen what happens when the forces aren't balanced and the organization falls from its lofty height.

Thrust

Thrust propels the organization forward but not necessarily toward an intended destination. That's one reason to use all aspects of the Model. Thrust not only propels you forward but allows the potential in Lift to get your organization off the ground.

Let's address the primary phases in which you use Thrust. At the appropriate time, be careful to only apply the Thrust required to position your organization for takeoff. For example, multiple organizations "crashed" during the "dot com" bust because they applied too much Thrust before they were ready to manage the scope of issues required to run a business. Many of these companies had great ideas but not much in place to execute their lofty ideas.

Once you're prepared for flight, you need to introduce enough Thrust to allow that potential Lift to become actual. It's this phase of reaching "cruising altitude" that requires the most Thrust. If you've ever worked for a startup or launched a new product, you understand how difficult the situation is until you start receiving reorders or find a high percentage of new customers due to word-of-mouth advertising.

Let's make a direct connection between Thrust and leadership. Thrust is created through:

+ alignment of systems and goals

+ coordinated efforts

+ interdependent crews in operation

+ proper/best use of equipment/supplies/facilities, etc.

+ use of raw/direct materials consistent with specifications

+ quality control built into jobs and tasks

+ removal of waste and distractions

+ optimal support crew able to manage the needs of the primary producers

Like Lift, Thrust requires a True Leader to ensure the organization operates successfully. Because it requires coordinated group as well as individual efforts, Thrust produces *effective* results.

Here's the Thrust caveat: *If you aren't careful, you could go too slow or too fast.* You need to carefully plan the speed of your organization to match multiple factors, especially accurately measuring supply and demand.

As described, Lift and Thrust might appear to be common sense. Yet optimal Lift and Thrust are not common in practice. As you learn to become a Great Leader, using both Lift and Thrust to your greatest advantage is key.

Drag and Weight: Forces that Hold Us Back and Keep Us Down

Drag

Drag holds us back and usually results from *ineffectiveness.*

Primarily, Drag includes the negative side of most of the aspects offered for Thrust and some of those mentioned about Lift, namely:

+ unproductive meetings

+ poor/non-existent communication

+ poor/non-existent training and development

+ lack of focus on the current/future marketplace

+ lack of monitoring trends

+ a hodge-podge of systems/goals even though there often seems to be a plethora of activity

+ little or no trust among the members who become divided into "camps"

 (Is a mind picture forming of one or more places you have worked?)

Drag must be overcome with greater-than-necessary Lift and Thrust, which wastes valuable resources. Here's the Drag caveat: What might be considered the job of an organization's Devil's Advocate is to hold you back—which can be good. For example, the typical military structure is quite hierarchical. That's why those "lower in rank" to the leader might be unwilling to offer their ideas and opinions. They acquiesce to the leader. Most of the well-functioning military units I had the honor to be a part of each had a capable leader willing to make and support the final decisions. But these leaders did everything they could to ensure the crew recognized how important their individual contributions were.

Along those lines, many years ago, a mentor taught me how to ensure people recognize that I value their input. That meant having a Devil's Advocate reporting directly to me in a position of authority. In some organizations, this is not only a good idea but necessary to protect that person from office politics.

The job of the Devil's Advocate, either openly or behind closed doors (depending on the arrangement between the leader and the Devil's Advocate), is to guarantee the organization considers what you're doing and how you're doing it. We often find the Devil's Advocate becomes a key source of intelligence. Why? Because many crew members will, at least initially, be more willing to talk openly with the Devil's Advocate than you, the leader (and their boss).

Minimizing "groupthink" and encouraging individual input from your crew (not only the bosses) can be the make-or-break aspect of your organization. So find at least one internal antagonist to prevent groupthink. Be careful, though; the intent is not to tag the most negative person. Rather, choose someone who has the organization's best interest at heart and the intestinal fortitude to take on this role.

In larger organizations, having more than one Devil's Advocate helps ensure one person doesn't take all the grief. In a perfect world, this would not be necessary, but I've seen situations in which the plan falls apart, usually from a lack of a clear understanding and expectations. I'm not proud of it, but I was guilty of this on at least two occasions.

If you are in doubt, establish a relationship in which the Devil's Advocate consults with you in private until you both reach a level of comfort when openly challenging the organization's path is warranted.

Get the Most from a Devil's Advocate

For other than the strongest and most confident, the job can feel like the person is constantly flying into strong headwinds. Consider rotating the role among those who can handle it. If you're unable to find someone within the organization to fill this role or don't know how to get the most from an internal Devil's Advocate, hire a good coach with this in mind.

Weight/Dead Weight

Weight keeps us down and makes it harder to get off the ground and climb. (Look for Gravity, or what *pulls* us down, in External Conditions.)

What's Dead Weight? This includes anyone in your organization whose potential has not been Unlocked, Engaged, and Optimized. That said, don't start looking for the deadbeats in your organization. Although it's possible some crewmembers aren't pulling their weight, it's better to start by measuring the success (or lack thereof) on the part of the leaders. The Dead Weight of ineffective leaders and what they cause is primarily why organizations fail to live up to their potential. Therefore, this needs to be the first issue to resolve.

Dead Weight indicates the lack of a clear Vision and Mission or the crew's connection to both. Other things that cause Dead Weight are:

+ lack of respect

+ treating people as commodities

+ no true incentives to do a good job

+ plenty of incentives to do just enough not to get fired

Dead Weight must be compensated for by greater than normal Lift and Thrust, which can be both expensive and wasteful.

How much time do you spend dealing with the same issues every day? It might be due to Dead Weight, so consider what needs to be improved first.

Here is the Weight caveat: As the saying goes, being "grounded in reality" can be a good thing and doesn't relate to the issues listed as Dead Weight. Tools are available to ensure you stay grounded. Start with this exercise.

Look in the mirror and ask if the first or the second attitude is closer to the one you present to the people who work with/for you?

+ "I am indispensable; the organization wouldn't survive without me."

+ "I work hard to ensure I do everything I can to help our organization be successful; how might I help you?"

Being proud of the work you do is one thing. Being egotistical is another. Some people offer that the organization within which they work is so "political" the first attitude is both expected and required for survival. If this is true, why would talented leaders continue to operate in that environment? After all, it appears they aren't working to transform the organization but perpetuating the Scarcity Mentality mindset and culture.

In reality, though, we are all dispensable. Taken to the extreme, it's a natural part of the cycle of life. The first attitude creates Dead Weight because people are working to help themselves, not the crew. If you haven't already done so, adopt the second attitude.

If you can minimize the negative aspects of Drag and Weight, imagine the possibilities. What could that do for you and your organization? Would you like to increase your performance, decrease your use of resources, and significantly decrease the rate of turnover in your organization? Would you like to stay focused on achieving your Vision (and not be embroiled in "crap")? It can be a beautiful thing.

External Conditions

Be sure to recognize the External Conditions you have to deal with or avoid. First, let's look at what to avoid.

Thunderstorms

Depicted in the graphic for our Successful Ventures in Human Dynamics Model is one of the obvious things airplanes must avoid—thunderstorms. In the financial world, "thunderstorms" commonly occur, but that doesn't mean having to experience the effects of those storms. Begin to use the process of Achieving the Vision and get the help you need to get On Course. (This idea is derived from Napoleon Hill's book *Think and Grow Rich*, which I highly recommend.)

Used effectively, these techniques help you foresee the looming storms so you can set your course to avoid them and other issues. (In subsequent steps of the series, we'll explore other sources of help, such as forming a leader council.)

Wind

Perhaps only on blustery days do most landlubbers think about the phenomenon of wind. However, it was a factor in every flight I took, from determining the runway I could use for takeoff/landing, to proper navigation, the time it would take to get to my destination, and more. In the workplace, I equate Wind to aspects of business that are subject to change in both direction and intensity. A smattering of examples includes regulations, laws, resource availability, weakness in the Foundation for Success (discussed shortly), and so on.

Gravity

Another unavoidable External Condition is Gravity, the External Condition that continuously acts to pull you down. Many things fit this dynamic, a prime culprit being business competition. Similarly, understand the forces you need to balance as you work to become a Great Leader. Use the Model to help you improve your operations—both current and future.

Tactical Uses – Five Common Employee Concerns

Every situation or scenario I've explored has been improved by this Model. It can be used for both strategic and tactical applications. Let's look at some tactical issues in a simplified case-study format. We'll address five common employee concerns and compare the perspectives of an old-school company and a company using the new way.

Plus, let's set a baseline and assume both the old-school company and the new-way company have products and/or services that are currently in high demand. It's not likely the situation will last or that market share will be maintained without significant effort, but for the sake of the case study, let's assume that's true.

Perspective #1: Initial Training (Orientation)

A representative from the old-school organization might toss the new employee a large binder and say, "Here's the manual. Let me know what you don't understand." Did you scoff in disbelief as if this would never happen? It's closer to the norm than you might believe. The organization using the new way is likely to offer plenty of opportunities for the new employee to understand exactly what's expected of him/her. This often includes a quasi-mentor who offers, "Let me show you."

The old-school way induces Drag before the employee even starts. The new way provides Lift and possibly Thrust.

Perspective #2: Using a Crew Member's Skills

In interviews I've conducted in old-school companies, I ask, "What's it like working here?" and employees respond with either "I'm bored" or "I feel like I'm stealing my paycheck." The first of these excuses is Drag and the second is a form of Dead Weight.

Significantly different responses to the same questions happen in companies operating the new way compared with the old way. (Yes, these are actual statements people made.)

✦ "I'm so jazzed to come to work every day. I feel like I'm pushing the envelope of my capabilities."

✦ "It feels great to know how much I'm contributing to our operations."

Wouldn't you rather have the Lift and Thrust produced by these responses?

Perspective #3: Accepting a Crew Member's Input

Too many old-school operations treat their people like commodities. The "Do what I tell you" mindset is alive and well. Many employees in these organizations don't bother to offer input because they know it won't be accepted. In some organizations, it's even worse when employees have said, "Yeah, they asked for my input, but I swear they just put it in the circular file because I never heard another thing—nor was it implemented." Think of the Drag created by the first and the Dead Weight created by the second.

In organizations people like to work for, the responses are significantly different:

✦ "I've never worked for an organization that expected me to provide input before. At first I was nervous about it, but once I got used to it and realized the leaders wouldn't harm me in any way because of it, I really enjoy it. I feel like I'm part of the team."

✦ "Can you believe it; not only do they ask for my input, but I can take credit for a number of changes that have been enacted because of things I've offered."

Although I don't hear these responses often, it pleases me when I do. Folks, this is the Lift and Thrust you can have in your organization.

Perspective #4: Meetings

One of the most dreaded words in modern business is meetings—"where minutes are kept and hours are lost." In reality, meetings can be quite productive. When asking people working in organizations with the old-school mindset how productive meetings are in their organization, two general comments are:

+ "If anyone really measured, they would realize our meetings result in negative ROI [Return on Investment]"

+ "They're a waste of time. And not just mine, but all the customers I can't help when I'm stuck in stupid, boring meetings."

If I were the leader in these organizations, I'd certainly want to reduce this Drag and Dead Weight. Instead, I'd feel compelled to do something that would make this the norm:

+ "Our meetings serve as incredibly positive communication channels."

+ "I can, without a doubt, rate our meetings as incredibly productive."

We need more Lift and Thrust from meetings, but how do we get them?

An excellent resource is Patrick Lencioni's *Death by Meeting*. (See Appendix D.) Patrick does a great job of turning a difficult topic into story form, which makes the information easy to read, understand,

and implement. He provides a useful outline of different types of meetings and how to lead them. Andy Grove also offers good ideas in his book *High Output Management,* mentioned previously. Check out these resources to help you and your organization overcome the pain of meetings many go through. More important, properly led meetings help the organization achieve its Vision.

Perspective #5: Rewards

One of the biggest problems with the reward structures in organizations is that leaders assume too much. Would-Be Leaders (Wanna-Be and False Leaders) believe reward options are insignificant. Great Leaders realize it's difficult to create one-size-fits-all reward plans that will incentivize everyone in the workforce.

Comments from the folks who work in old-school organizations include:

+ "I'm not sure there's a connection to my performance."

+ "I wasn't sure how to answer your question because for the kind of work they require of me, I don't believe I get anything I would classify as a reward. Sure, I get my paycheck, but it doesn't adequately compensate me for what I'm expected to accomplish."

For responses similar to the second entry, I ask this follow-up question: "Then why do you stay here?" The response is typically one of these:

+ "Trust me, as soon as I find another job, I'm out of here," or

✦ "It's the economy, man. I have to feed my kids and so
   I'll keep this job. But as soon as the economy turns
   around, I'll be looking for something else."

Wouldn't you be dismayed if those responses came from employees who worked with you!

It doesn't have to be this way. When rewards are less than ade-
quate, you lose effectiveness in your operations. When work is unreasonable, people working with/for you lose focus and desire. Here's
what people from organizations using the new way say:

✦ "I think this is the first place I've worked where the people in charge really do seem to take notice of the extra
   work I do and do their best to reward me for it," and

✦ "The bosses come through. If we meet our goals,
   we're rewarded appropriately. If we exceed our goals,
   rewards are commensurate."

Now consider External Conditions. Whether they're working
through headhunters or directly, your competitors are continually
searching for the best-of-the-best—vital to every organization. In
another scenario, let's assume the compensation schedule is similar between an old-school organization and one using the new way.
When a competing new-way organization contacts people working
for/with an old-school organization, would the company's employees be likely to explore the option of jumping ship? The answer is
obvious. Turnover is expensive, not only in dollars but talent, experience, and other intangibles. That's to be considered when employees
leave due to the organization being poorly led. It's another reason to
turn the company around.

A Macro Perspective

In case you're wondering if the Model works only on the micro perspective of organizations, let's look at it from a macro perspective that affects people around the world. The founding of the United States was the advent that allowed this fledgling country to eventually be more On Course and soar higher than any other throughout history. I don't say that out of arrogance but out of reality. As mentioned previously, this country has never been perfect, but in terms of its On Net impact around the world, there must have been a reason that happened.

After studying U.S. history and that of other countries (especially so-called great societies), I believe the Vision of our founders pointed the plane (i.e., our country) in a desired direction and provided the Lift it needed. Our people accepted the challenge. Thousands of dynamic innovators provided the Thrust that resulted in grand accomplishments. One of those was lifting more people out of poverty than any other country/economic structure throughout human history.

Unfortunately, as noted earlier, the country is Off Course today. The Lift and Thrust are still there, but we've added Drag and Weight. It's up to those who desire to increase peace, freedom, and prosperity for all people worldwide to make it happen. We can either do our best to reduce Drag and Weight or—not as efficient—compensate by increasing both Lift and Thrust.

The key to getting back On Course is to follow the Lessons of the Geese. (If you don't know this term, Google it, watch the video, and adopt it into your modus operandi.) These lessons imply if we cooperate the way geese do when in formation, we can soar even higher.

A caution: Following just any leader is dangerous. As the Asch Elevator Conformity experiment shows, many people will follow the crowd for a number of reasons. I encourage you to watch this vid-eo on the Asch Elevator Conformity experiment.[21][22] It shows what happens when too many follow the crowd. Do what you know is right; don't merely follow the crowd. Follow only True Leaders and become a True Leader.

To improve your ability to use the Model, next you'll learn about the 5 Prime Values and the Foundation for Success. They will help you point your plane in the desired direction and do your part to ensure Lift is available for all. What are they?

1. *The 5 Prime Values:* To start out On Course (i.e., get your Heading Indicator pointed North), you would adopt and employ each of these Prime Values. The key: Consistency with these values.

2. *The Foundation for Success:* These five pillars can facilitate your own Heading Indicator by helping you determine if you've pointed your plane in the desired direction. When explored collectively, these same pillars help determine if our society is providing the Lift that's desperately needed. The five pillars are vital for the success of all people. The key: *We can't assume it's all someone else's job.*

chapter eight
THE 5 PRIME VALUES

T he challenges to becoming a True Leader include fixing our current problems and then tackling the challenge of achieving the next level of the human condition. This will require that we understand, adopt, and consistently employ the 5 Prime Values addressed in this chapter.

The term "values" can have multiple meanings. This discussion defines it as: *Those beliefs and priorities you follow to determine how you live and work.* A caution: We can and should talk about these, but it's how we use them that's vital.

KiVisions Value Statements

KiVisions has two value statements derived by deeply exploring the 5 Prime Values. We offer ours as examples as you create your own.

One value statement guides our relationships with those external to our company: *We work to ensure Mutual Respect, Prosperity, and Growth.*

> The other statement guides our internal relationships: *We commit to maintaining what holds us together, our TRUE-Glue: Trust, Respect, Understanding, and Expectations.*
>
> We'll discuss each of these values as we work through the series.

Origin of the 5 Prime Values

My friend Donna Maria Robinson helped me understand that to lead the richest, most fulfilling, and satisfying life possible, we're called to *Love, Learn, Live, Laugh,* and *Leave a Legendary Legacy*—the 5 Values. True Leaders who adopt and employ these values develop the ability to proactively prevent problems and not just solve those that occur.

Primarily, these values are stated as verbs because you need to put them into action. How well you follow each value helps determine whether your Heading Indicator points North. Secondarily, these values used as nouns represent potential (think Lift). How closely you live in accordance with these values determines how fulfilling your life has been, is, and will be.

Prime Value #1: Love

No, I haven't become a flower child. There's simply no greater gift than love—the deep, abiding affection you have for other human beings. You love them if you want the best for them and care what happens to them. A love for people shouldn't be confused with affection, but you'll likely find it difficult to separate the two. Love is the reason I strongly believe in the Abundance Mentality. The Scarcity Mentality (I Win) offers a selfish view of the world. The Abundance Mentality (We Win) provides a view that might be uncommon but critical. It promotes the value of serving my needs by helping others with theirs.

My understanding of this topic comes from growing up with seven brothers and sisters and now having a beautiful family of my own. What I most learned from my family— the one abundant thing that connects us—is love. Eventually, I came to understand the value of working together to accomplish things, great and small. Love is the glue.

Two cautions: For those closest to you, try not to dis-love them because of the frustrations you experience in the normal course of human interactions. And do your best not to discount others far away. Reasons for separation from others—physical and geographical barriers—can be resolved, even for those living abroad.[23] However, differences in values—that is, how you see and operate in the world—will likely be a challenge for True Leaders to tackle in the workplace.

The value of love is a powerful facilitator of human relationships. When we understand it and use it as intended, we interact in positive ways. If we fail to understand it or lose it, our interactions are usually negative and sometimes depressingly so. Remember, I'm promoting this as a value, not an emotion in the way you love others: family, friends, and coworkers.

When you truly love people, you engage them not only on business and organizational issues but on what's affecting them personally. Personal issues carry over directly to the workplace. It's not about serving as a counselor but rather about realizing the potential for *using* counselors to help your people deal with personal issues such as financial difficulties, addictions, and the like. Pay attention not only to their issues but to those of family members so they can focus their time at work on work.

Is this an upfront investment? Sure. But such a move absolutely provides positive returns. It will also help overcome the negative connotation of the word *boss*. If you do this as prescribed and can prove how well it works for your people and organization, I'll buy you dinner as my way of saying thanks for taking the risk. You want fries with that?

The following issues can cause difficulty if you don't maintain your self-control.

Like: Avoid confusing "liking" with "loving." As a value, loving is a choice we make; I'm not sure liking someone involves much choice. Some people I don't like very much, but because they're humans, I do love them and hope we can be civil with each other. Liking is often a natural reaction to any number of factors, including what people say or do.

At the various medical centers where I worked, I chose many of the people who worked *for* me but not many who worked *with* me. Some had values that weren't similar to mine. I could have allowed this difference to affect achieving the Vision. On reflection, I came to realize those people were likely struggling as much as I was. Fortunately, in most situations, we achieved the Vision by finding compromises to ensure the organization's success.

Lust: Those high school science classes you slept through might have come in handy to understand this one. It's natural to be physically attracted to certain other humans. Check yourself and don't fall prey to animal-like instincts. Oh, the problems they can cause…. (Do I sense a reluctance to even address this one?)

Before cell phones, the three fastest forms of communication had been telegraph, telephone, and tell-a-medic. Hospitals can be an amazing source of gossip—some fabricated and some real. As an example, a young married man I'll call George worked for me and did his job at the hospital well. Through the grapevine, I heard he was involved with a woman who also worked there but not for me directly. I'm not sure why I failed to address this situation shortly after I found out. But the dirty details started filtering up to me, which implies they were rampant in levels below the executive suite.

I began to notice changes. George became less engaged with the rest of the staff who worked for me, which hindered communication and productivity. He and his wife quit attending functions to promote the facility. It became obvious (without saying anything) that senior staff members were less willing to accept proposals George offered. Bottom line: George became less effective than he had been. And this addresses only George's professional side. I can only imagine the effect on his family and all those affiliated with the woman involved.

By the time I felt compelled to address this issue with George, he told me the affair had been over for a while. Would it have made a difference had I brought it up earlier? Maybe, but I learned from this experience to at least try.

As a leader, do your best to decide if and how to address such issues when they arise. They can cause distrust and lack of respect while distracting from good order and discipline in your organization.

Obsession: When others recognize that love of humans is something we value, the rewards can be great. Among the best are connections with others. Among the worst are connections with others that fly out of balance.

Here's an example of a situation. A colleague I'll call Marcus shared a story about a co-worker I'll call him Ethan. Marcus had mentored Ethan, who was more than grateful for the help. He seemed to believe Marcus had achieved god-like status. The obsession involved daily in-person visits (not normal for the situation), phone calls, and other communications that went beyond appropriate. (From my perspective this wasn't a paranoid rant from Marcus.) Fortunately, Ethan was due to be moved to another medical facility many miles away. After his departure, the obsession waned.

I offer this to make you aware of the possibility. Sometimes, receiving a god-like status can play to the ego. Some people have even allowed their "fans" to provide them with inappropriate gifts. If you're caught in a situation like this, be careful and be smart.

More Right Questions. To develop your Vision and become a True Leader, let's delve into more Right Questions.

✦ *Who is most important to you?* You're probably willing to explore a Vision you hope to provide for those closest to you or help them develop for themselves. But when should you keep guiding them, and when is it best to let them go? As a parent or boss, it's difficult to not only know when someone is ready for new challenges but also realize you can't protect them forever. As difficult as this may be with your kids, it can be just as difficult with your protégés. You need to discern when to let go so they can learn from experience yet can still turn to you when you're needed as a coach.

Leaders who operate with a Scarcity Mentality are often narcissists; they have an unhealthy belief they are the most important beings. Because they work hard to impress themselves, they often impress others—initially. Over time, their self-centered tendencies prove they are only interested in promoting their own well-being; they are not focused on helping others. This trait in a leader is hostile toward achieving a group's vision.

✦ *What is most important to you?* What are the key drivers in your life? Here's a driver for me that provides insight into why I do what I do: I love people, I hate waste. Human potential fits both of these drivers. Wasted potential results in suffering—and not just our own. Think of all the great things you might do to make somebody else's life better.

Keeping On Track

If you stay focused on your greatest challenge, it will keep you on track. In the 1960s, U.S. President John F. Kennedy gave a speech that galvanized the country toward what seemed like an impossible mission—reach the moon by the end of the decade. This Moon Shot became his famous challenge to the country.

Soviet cosmonaut Yuri Gagarin served as the prime catalyst for Kennedy's Moon Shot speech. On April 12, 1961, Yuri was the first human to journey into outer space aboard a Vostok spacecraft, successfully completing an orbit of the Earth.[24]

Was Kennedy's speech a result of pure competitiveness or did he fear the Soviets would use their space program to gain a military advantage over America? Regardless, it got America's collective butt in gear. A catalyst like this is often needed to spur people into action.

President Kennedy gave his formal "We choose to go to the moon" speech on September 12, 1962. On July 20, 1969, Neil Armstrong and Buzz Aldrin conducted the first walk by humans on the surface of the moon.

Now, you might scoff at suggesting that landing on the moon was a great historic achievement. What did it do to advance the position of humans? When you look at the technology that emerged and the merits of its broad applications, this Moon Shot catalyzed an incredible array of items that make a difference in our modern lives.[25] Just a few examples: light emitting diodes (LEDS), infrared ear thermometers, and artificial limbs.

Have you declared your Moon Shot, or are you waiting for your personal Gagarin to catalyze your action?

The KiVisions Leader Development Process addresses purpose and potential of leaders because a prime way to Unlock, Engage, and Optimize your potential is having a vision of what you're striving to achieve. If the people you lead, including yourself, are important to you (i.e., you love them), then help them find what *they* want to accomplish—their Moon Shot. Let both your love for them and what's important to you drive *you* to unlock, engage, and optimize your own potential.

Prime Value #2: Learn, Continuously

Many people believe they were given a pass to stop learning when they left school—whether that was high school, tech school, college, or another educational system. As contributing members of society, however, we must commit to learning throughout our lives. Those who believe they have a pass on learning are making a mistake.

Learning definitely helps unlock your potential as you adopt this mindset and guide others to find a similar path. A caution: "Learn, continuously" doesn't mean you can perpetually attend school as an excuse for not contributing anything meaningful to society.

Phase 2 of the Helping True Leaders Soar to Greatness series delves into the problems caused by those who aren't contributing. Continuous learning upgrades our skills; it doesn't help us escape our responsibilities. Ultimately, we need to apply what we're learning to help the world increase Peace, Freedom, and Prosperity.

"School" is not just a building; it requires us to open our minds to vast opportunities. Experience can be a great teacher, but as future phases of the series will define, we're best served if we don't blaze trails into territory that's already been confirmed. I accept that $1+1 = 2$, so there's no need to explore that concept further.

Why is continuous learning needed? Because humans are subject to the consequences of Creative Destruction—a term coined by Austrian-born American economist Joseph Schumpeter. He defined it as the "process of industrial mutation that incessantly revolutionizes the economic structure from within, incessantly destroying the old one, incessantly creating a new one."[26] That's why buggy whip manufacturers went out of business after the automobile introduced an innovative way to get from point A to point B.

Many lives have been significantly disrupted, if not damaged, when people didn't recognize the changes on the horizon and prepare accordingly. That's why it's critical to stay ahead of the curve and ensure we have the skills, talent, and temperament to succeed in the future world, not just the present.

The Importance of Being Ahead of the Curve

"Ahead of the curve" represents a statistical placement on a bell curve. At a minimum, you work to ensure you are at the top of the curve or right of the midpoint.

If you went to college, it was common for you and your friends to discuss the effort required in a class to get the grade you desired. To be above average, therefore, your grades would have to be to the right of the midpoint of the bell curve.

Aviation has a similar issue. Pilots hope to be *ahead of the power curve.* I won't get too technical here, but the power curve concept maintains that below a specific airspeed, maintaining that speed counter-intuitively requires *more* Thrust rather than less Thrust. The consequences of being "behind the curve" can be disastrous. In this situation, it's necessary to balance Lift, Thrust, and Drag.

Learning and Employment. One of the indexes used to measure the health of our economy (from the JOLT Survey), the Unemployment Index, should be supplemented with the Unemployable Index. Using both might provide a clearer picture of the job situation in the country. Under what the Fed considers "slack labor conditions" (that is, lots of people looking for jobs), how is it possible we can have an incredible number of jobs available? As I write this, over five million jobs in the U.S. are listed as unfilled. What's the only reasonable answer? Organizations with available jobs are having a difficult time finding people capable of performing those jobs to the standards their leaders set.

How can we help people understand the need to learn continuously? True Leaders encourage others to realize they have much to contribute. They help them unlock, engage, and optimize their potential by being open to possibilities—by taking every opportunity to observe, reflect, hypothesize, and attempt to prove things that are important to them.

What Do You Read and How Much?

How many books do you read in a year? Are they graphic novels or tomes with substance?

I'm a convert. Instead of reading only what was necessary to help me survive the day, I now spend hours attempting to absorb the myriad lessons others offer. Topics dealing with leader development top my list, but I don't want to be a "one-trick pony" so I peruse a variety of subjects.

I also explore books related to the brands of our company: teaching, mentoring, coaching, and consulting. Plus, I run a business and look to others for recommendations on how to handle business activities as successfully as possible.

Within the last few years, my newest books will help qualify me as a "man of the world." One of them was eye-opening *Tao Te Ching* by Lao Tzu.[27] Although I will not claim to fully understand all his ideas, it helped me realize I must never believe I have reached the fullness of my potential. This passage provides an example: "The Tao is (like) the emptiness of a vessel; and in our employment of it we must be on our guard against all fullness."

Learning and Teaching. Prime Value #2 (Learn, continuously) connects directly with one of the components of the Foundation for Success addressed in the next chapter. A key reflection is understanding that teaching doesn't always require having a teaching certificate. No, I'm not saying we accept anybody off the street in our school systems. Rather, let's recognize a key to growth is learning to deal effectively with the different perspectives put forth by others. For example, sometimes people believe "qualified to teach" requires the teacher be older than the students—a mistake. People of any age can help us understand things.

Learning and Engagement. Two key questions: 1) What do you know about your organization? and 2) Where do you get your information?

More leaders need to get out and about, not just perform "fly-by scootings." This refers to those Would-Be leaders who believe if people throughout their organization see their faces once in a while, it's sufficient. Instead, spend time with your crew, your customers, your vendors, your union reps, and so on. Stay engaged with the folks who help ensure your vision is achieved.

Does the First Amendment of the Bill of Rights to the U.S. Constitution—free speech—still have merit? Some would shut down debate on any number of topics—supposedly to "protect" others' sensibilities. What a huge mistake! Rather, those who claim a need for tolerance of others' opinions are on the right track.

As part of the learning process, we need to be open to the thoughts and ideas of others. But that doesn't mean we necessarily have to like or buy in to their ideas and behaviors. As Voltaire, the French Enlightenment writer, offered, "I do not agree with what you have to say, but I'll defend to the death your right to say it." Those who attempt to shut down free speech for their own gain are concerning. They come across as tolerating all opinions as long as those opinions match their own. We don't learn to deal with each other effectively by shutting people up.

Yes, some limits are reasonable. We can't falsely yell "fire" in a crowded theater, but we can't tolerate the standard that no one can say something that offends someone else. Here's a reality check: *We'll be offended more than once in our lifetime, but let's allow that offense to help us grow.* This lesson was hard for me to accept, but it's helped me immensely.

Falling into this category is bias or "news with an agenda." Don't be led into believing only the "other side" is biased—another example of the Sports Team Mindset discussed previously. I have fairly strong feelings on most issues. As a voter, I'm a registered Independent. Part of this decision is due to a friend who helped me understand the value of opening myself to the opinions of those I agreed with and also *disagreed* with. I used to force myself to read accounts that went against my existing opinions. Now it's second nature and quite refreshing to read a variety of opinions. It helps me understand others and clarify my beliefs in the process.

Prime Value #3: Live

Do you live or merely exist, moving from distraction to distraction but never truly living? To determine your priorities, devise a plan on how you will accomplish your goals and review them to determine if you are On Course.

With all the distractions, opportunities, and challenges in this world, it's difficult to stay focused. Yet something grand inside you just waits to come out. Get past it and jump the next hurdle, knowing you have the ability to accomplish that grand purpose. It becomes truly overwhelming for many folks.

Also ask, "Which do you want: to be more fulfilled or to have a life filled with more stuff?" They're not the same, and it goes back to the distractions. Too many people measure success by the toys they have. But how do those toys prove you've done something great?

Let's be careful that material things used to represent success don't clutter our lives so we're always dealing with the stuff we *have* rather than the true successes we might *achieve*. Live—whether you become a progenitor or pro-janitor. Find something both useful and necessary to others.

Progenitor: a person who begins something.

I'm asking you to help us get back On Course. As a True Leader, you can help begin the process of getting us closer to "yes" on each of the 5 Key Questions addressed earlier. Be a progenitor, help ignite the flame of the RAVOlUtion (see Chapter 9).

Let's examine four issues that relate to living: adversity, competition, opportunities, and money.

Adversity: Like those quests you vicariously observe, your own may be steeped in adversity: danger, toil, hardship, and the like. The reality: You don't know for sure if what you're doing will ultimately yield success, but you know it's your path. You walk it and greet each challenge with the most strength you can.

A key to living this way is combining some of the values already presented. Thus, if you Love and Learn, you will likely find greater success as you Live.

Competition: Do you know your limits? Have you pushed the envelope?

Pushing the Envelope

This phrase has its origins in the world of aviation. Since the late 1960s, the word envelope in aviation has meant a set of performance limits that may not be safely exceeded. To "push the envelope" implies you're searching for your actual limits—maybe because you know you have greater potential inside you waiting to come out.

Until you've pushed your envelope, how will you know your true capabilities? That's not to imply you should necessarily exceed your limits, but it's exactly what I recommend to certain clients. They especially apply to those with whom I have a close relationship, and I know they won't crash and burn. Even, and maybe especially, if you've always succeeded with high marks, chances are you have more inside waiting to be unlocked.

Fly Higher

The path Seth Godin recommended in his book *The Icarus Deception: How High Will You Fly?* (see Appendix D) is worth pondering. Icarus crashed to his death because he supposedly flew too close to the sun, melting the wax that affixed the feathers of his wings. Godin offers that we're taught the dangers of "flying too high" but never the dangers of flying too low. His advice: "Fly higher!"—that is, Unlock, Engage, and Optimize your potential.

But don't assume that because you failed at something, you've found your limits. Explore why you failed. If you gave it all you had, you may have found a *current* limit in that arena. But that doesn't mean you shouldn't attempt to do more in other arenas—or even in that one at a different time. Education, experience, and coaching can expand your envelope so what had been unattainable is now within reach.

If you failed but know you didn't give it all you had, explore why. It may be you weren't truly passionate about it, or you were distracted by a higher or, heaven forbid, lower priority. In fact, to fully Unlock, Engage, and Optimize your potential *requires* failure. As IBM founder Tom Watson claimed, "Success is on the far side of failure."

Once you set your targets (results, effect, dollars, etc.), determine if you have the natural diligence and discipline to execute your plan. Be competitive. If you need a "foil" with whom to compete, that's fine, but get to the point of your greatest competitor being yourself. Set unrealistic goals and do your best to achieve them.

However, make sure your BHAGs (Big Hairy Audacious Goals coined by Collins and Porras in *Built to Last*[28]) are based on your true priorities. At the same time, be careful in the commitments you make. Don't abandon people who count on you or your other priorities to achieve one goal at the expense of another.

Opportunities: Sometimes great opportunities are presented as anything but great. Receiving my United States military draft notice was a source of dread. On many days, I wasn't sure I'd be going home. On other days, I felt alone and longed to be with my family. I was pushed harder than ever before, digging deep to find strength for the next step. But, looking back, I wouldn't trade that experience for having a cushier life.

Money: It provides an easy comparison but a poor indicator of our true worth. Treat money as a tool used for living. As a friend helped me realize, we shouldn't judge our insides by others' outsides—including their show of wealth.

Lots of people become severely depressed by their lack of financial wealth. They falsely believe that because they don't have the same "toys" as others, they're doing something wrong. In most of these cases, they learn to recognize they might be making sound decisions by not going into debilitating debt. When I tracked a few supposedly successful people, I found almost everyone was living well beyond his or her means.

What can you do? Help people who are discouraged to realize the progress they've made on their short-term goals. Suggest they might need better short-term targets to reach their long-term goals. Find things other than expensive toys to help you recognize you're likely more On Course than those who have the expensive toys.

In his book *Stop Acting Rich and Start Living like a Real Millionaire* (see Appendix D), Dr. Thomas Stanley says the vast majority of people who own and drive luxury cars are not millionaires. Dr. Stanley recommends following the wisdom of living within your means. If you find something you want, earn the money first and then go buy it!

Prime Value #4: Laugh and Celebrate Life!

The value of laughter is about celebrating life and enjoying the struggle. If your youth was anything like mine, you often heard, "Suck it up; you'll be a better person and feel much better about yourself in the future because of the trials and tribulations you go through today." I hated that advice—but now I recognize its truth. It reminds me of another phrase, attributed to our Amish friends: "Too soon old, too old smart."

Some people celebrate without achieving anything worth celebrating. Others are so focused on achieving, they simply move on to the next goal when the previous one is accomplished. Be realistic about what you celebrate. Don't give everyone a trophy for showing up. However, understand that some people need you to recognize real accomplishments (especially their part in them) before they can mentally move on to the next goal.

In addition to celebrating the highs, you'll likely experience bumps in the road or even devastating events. It's amazing how many people I know were "living the life" until a close associate pulled the rug out from under them—in this case, by stealing. That situation led many of my friends to seek bankruptcy. It's not fun, but it's life.

Watch, listen to, or read Tony Robbins or Brendon Burchard, both of whom openly talk about their situations. For a time, Tony was forced to do his dishes in the bathtub because there was no sink in the apartment he could afford. Brendon moved in with his girlfriend to reduce expenses. He used their bedroom as his office and their bed as his filing cabinet. Today, you'd never guess they've had a bad day in their lives. They're positive and energetic. They've shortened their days of depression by looking forward and become great role models in this regard.

Like these men did, make lemonade out of those lemons you encounter.

KiVisions Motto

(Which you're welcome to adopt)

Make Monday something you and your crew look forward to.

Regardless of whether you're an over- or under-celebrator, pick something you want to achieve. When you achieve that victory or milestone, celebrate it—appropriately. In addition, you can enhance the results your crew achieves when you, as the leader, recognize their accomplishments.

Laugh *at* yourself and *with* others. It's okay to laugh at your own jokes. Others may not get them, but that's okay. What some might call quirks help define us.

Prime Value #5: Leave a Legendary Legacy

What's the incredible potential deep inside you? Have you committed to achieving what you've been called to do?

Consider values to be ways of being you commit to, that guide the way you live. You have to work hard to incorporate those values into your daily actions, but committing to them is important. Still, you can live a fulfilling life that produces results if you adopt each of the 5 Prime Values.

To achieve your Vision, create a picture of the success you've chosen. Make it a grand quest. You might encounter pitfalls along the way, but when that point comes in your life to sit and reflect on your successes, they will enrich your story.

Some people talk about the value of writing your epitaph and striving to make it come true. When I was first introduced to this idea, I was learning to facilitate a course to help people adopt Dr. Stephen Covey's 7 Habits of Highly Effective People. This epitaph idea seemed morbid at the time and I couldn't wrap my head around it. Instead, I adopted a different approach—that is, I became a storyteller.

Here's the key: Once you've determined the legend you want to achieve, do everything you can to make it come true. Become your favorite legendary character, the Frodo Baggins of your time. (Frodo is a character in Tolkien's *Lord of the Rings* trilogy who not only survived but achieved his quest on a perilous adventure.)

Craft a wonderful life story that your kids, grandkids, and others will choose to pass down. You are called to Love, Learn, Live, Laugh, and Leave a Legendary Legacy. Once you're defined by these values, you're on your way to becoming a True Leader and living a more fulfilling life. Point your Heading Indicator North.

THE FOUNDATION FOR SUCCESS

This chapter might appear to depart from the scope of my work helping good people become Great Leaders at individual and organizational levels. However, for our society to get back On Course, a vital connection needs to be made. My rationale: Each aspect of the Foundation for Success has some measure of effect on every person and organization. I hope to help others realize the need to be *good Foundation* stewards, which is essential to the advancement of peace, freedom, and prosperity for all. We have both a primary role—the contributions we make by achieving our purpose—and a secondary role— contributing to the advancement of the Foundation in whatever aspect we deem appropriate.

5 Pillars of the Foundation for Success

The Foundation for Success either creates Lift and Thrust or Drag and Weight. The 5 Pillars making up the Foundation must function effectively for our society to remain On Course. Each pillar has aspects that require our attention as well as factors over which we have some influence but little control.

The 5 Pillars include unifying vision, health, education, energy, and governance.

1. *Unifying Vision:* Because of the current state of the human condition, this is necessary for the proper function of all groups. We may disagree on how to accomplish the vision, but we need something the vast majority can work collaboratively to achieve—something that unifies us such as President Kennedy's Moon Shot.

2. *Health:* This pillar exemplifies the idea of both internal and external aspects. Internal: to live a healthy life requires subscribing to a valid list of do's (e.g., exercise, diet, etc.) and don'ts (e.g., smoking, inappropriate alcohol use, illicit drugs, etc.). External: We depend on others who provide things we take for granted in our daily lives (e.g., the water that comes out of our tap) and healthcare experts who can help resolve issues we encounter.

3. *Education:* This connects to Prime Value #2: Learn, continuously. But the Education pillar also includes the formal processes for primary, secondary, and higher education systems that need revitalization.

4. *Energy:* Most of us live in an advanced society. As a microcosm example, medical centers could never provide the quality of care deemed standard without reliable energy. Few of us are involved in its production, but we have significant influence over the energy we use.

5. *Governance:* Governance bodies need our help, support, and oversight, and I'm not referring solely to government here. A prime example relates to Prime Value #2: Learn, continuously and Foundation Pillar #3: Education. Most likely, you live in an area where a school board oversees the primary and secondary education process. Do you assume school board members knowledgably and effectively use the resources needed for students to become well-educated? Well, don't assume.

Before going through each of the pillars, a caveat: As much as I'm convinced of the need to concentrate our efforts on each of these aspects, I'm not an expert in any of them. This discussion gets us thinking about the relevant pieces, and I hope that part of the necessary re-engagement happens here. We must ensure each pillar serves to provide Lift and Thrust, not the Drag and Weight we experience too often.

As we address each pillar with enough depth to stimulate personal reflection regarding action, I hope enough leaders accept the challenge to reclaim our country's position as the "shining city on the hill." That means helping the people of America live fulfilling lives and serve as humble role models for people around the world.

Unifying Vision

What is our unifying vision as a country? It's sad to think how far America has drifted from the days the Founding Fathers mutually pledged their "Lives, Fortunes, and Sacred Honor" (from the last sentence of the Declaration of Independence).

What proof do I offer that we've lost our vision? First, it's doubtful we can honestly answer yes to the 5 Key Questions asked at the beginning of this book. They are repeated and expanded on here.

To regain our course, Americans need to ensure we are:

1. On the cusp of a major breakthrough to heal what divides us while maintaining certain standards of conduct required by a reasonable, civil society.

2. As safe and secure as possible from threats to our health and way of life, while safeguarding freedom as a priority, not an afterthought.

3. Making decisions that are keeping us on a bright path to greater prosperity. (A key tenet: Ensure our youth are given the opportunity and understand the incentive to prepare to tackle life's challenges.)

4. Willing to testify to the value of everything we produce and the services we provide.

5. Soaring to our preferred future by living fulfilling lives and making significant contributions.

Having a Unifying Vision is a powerful tool to Unlock, Engage, and Optimize human potential.

Health

Like each of the components in the Foundation, our relative health touches on each of the 5 Key Questions and includes these issues:

General Health: Who is responsible for your health? The answer should be obvious, but unfortunately it's not. As a healthcare administrator, I encountered numerous people who believed their health was solely the responsibility of the healthcare system to which they belonged. They took no responsibility for personal actions that led to their current condition. Medical science is amazing, but it's not a panacea. Instead of divesting the responsibility to others, you need to reclaim primary responsibility and accept the consequences of the decisions you make in all facets of your life, including your health. It helps your Heading Indicator point North. Which of these important aspects require your attention?

Physical Health: The formula is simple; the application is not. Throughout my life, coaches have taught me the primary items on my to-do list: balance nutrition, keep well hydrated, get plenty of rest, and maintain endurance/flexibility/strength. Yes, the last requires a disciplined regimen of exercise. I also get an annual physical, and I trust my physician to catch things I might have missed that can be corrected.

Mental Health: Too few people talk about this subject openly. It's likely thousands need help but are currently unwilling or unable to get it. It's incumbent upon leaders to remove the negative stigma about mental health. Anyone unsure of his or her own mental state can get help. I had the fortune in my operational healthcare days to work with practitioners who did amazing work to help people deal with their mental issues.

Spiritual Health: Many of us feel blessed to have a religion we practice and would love to have others join our respective communities. However, a number of good people say they're quite spiritual but don't practice any particular religion. This is a personal choice. I can only offer what works for me. I'm human and, as such, I'm prone to make less than satisfactory decisions without a compass to guide me. Although I'm on a lifelong quest to improve my decision-making, I would have made many more mistakes without the spiritual compass of my religion.

Emotional Health: Sometimes managing our emotional health is confused with managing our mental health. Here's how I separate the two: I believe a mental health problem is the result of a condition, usually biological or physiological, for which we might need help and support from the mental health community. Like our physical health, much of our emotional health is based on the decisions we make. We need to find balance. If we push ourselves too little or too much, that's likely to negatively affect our emotional health. That may well be one of the reasons for the increasing number of life coaches in our world today. (Note: I'm a Certified Leader Coach, not a life coach.) Many people are looking for someone to help them find that balance. We can certainly maintain our physical health. Many people are so driven, they forget to take time for themselves and their health.

A coach who has helped me, Brendon Burchard, offers a program called High Performance Academy. One of his tips for life balance is to work in fifty-minute increments. Take ten minutes at the end of each fifty-minute segment to do things as simple as stand up, stretch, drink water, and so on. I get much more done when I follow this prescription. A number of coaches recommend building in time off and periodically getting away from the daily grind. Some completely turn off the computer for a week, spend time enjoying nature, visit with family and friends, etc. Find what works for you. Chances are you, too, will be more productive as a result of taking a complete break.

Environment: Foundation stewards pay attention to the environment. Whether it's drainage from mines in Pennsylvania or the EPA-caused spill in the Animas River in Colorado, we need to hold accountable those responsible. And no, an official or bureaucrat who stands up and says, "I'm sorry. I take full responsibility" doesn't absolve the person or the organization. It isn't sufficient. For example, Flint Michigan's water troubles in 2015–2016 should serve as a wake-up call. This crisis shows why it's important to stay engaged in life. It's difficult to live in peace, freedom, and prosperity when you can't safely drink the tap water.

People make mistakes, but we need to have negative consequences for mistakes that affect the rest of us—especially when they aren't corrected quickly or, worse, covered up. We've made too much progress on our air, water, and soil quality over the last few decades to allow backsliding into the filth of yesteryear. Because of that progress, reasonable standards have been put in place. (See EPA report "Progress Cleaning the Air and Improving People's Health."[29])Reliable enforcement of those standards must follow. Good news: Even the rivers in Pittsburgh have recovered enough that bass fishing tournaments commonly occur!

We can make a difference when we care and get involved. This is why I ask you to accept a role in maintaining and improving this Foundation for Success.

Education

Our children spend a good chunk of their lives preparing for what they'll do in the workplace. Are we teaching them the right way? When we compare our results to the rest of the world (especially considering the U.S. spends more per pupil than other countries), we see results that aren't commensurate with the effort. For example, the U.S. ranks well below most developed and even many underdeveloped countries in math, reading, and science.[30]

Let's look seriously at what our education system is doing. The often spouted bromide "spend more" is not likely the answer. Research has indicated the Federal Department of Education has failed to improve outcomes.[31] Maybe it's time to return the responsibility and money to each state. This will increase the accountability for those outcomes—especially when tied into each governor's tacit responsibility to ensure an environment that attracts lucrative jobs. Having a well-educated workforce goes a long way.

Role of Teachers: After teaching at Penn State for decades, I can speak about education with credentials. Good teachers can make a subject as difficult as accounting palatable and increase the probability of comprehension using the right effort and effective tools. A similar approach needs to be taken throughout our educational process. We need to look at best practices and learn more from experts such as Clayton Christensen, Curtis W. Johnson, and Michael B. Horn. Their book *Disrupting Class: How Disruptive Innovation Will Change the Way the World Learns* is an eye opener. (See Appendix D.)

Other incredible pioneers are establishing viable programs in the confines of inner city charter schools.[32] Some claim it's not possible to replicate these results in large school systems. That may be true, but how will we know unless we try?

Learning Styles: In educating youth, we're leaving too many kids in the dust. As many of them become frustrated, it often leads to unhealthy activities. Each human has incredible potential, with too much of it being wasted.

In exploring how to ensure they have the opportunity and incentive to prepare for tackling life's challenges, let's understand how each person learns best. Although it's well known that people have various learning styles, too few educators fold this knowledge into classroom and out-of-classroom activities. I endorse the VARK concept (Visual, Auditory, Reading/Writing, and Kinesthetic) for learning styles as explained in "All Students Are Created Equally (and Differently)"[33] I find it is fairly simple to grasp and it recognizes that learning styles are preferences each person favors. When redesigning the class

I taught at Penn State, I used this concept to develop the delivery of the material. Students were able to pick the "tools" that best suited their preferences for learning. Although we did not test our results empirically, our catering to learning styles made a significant difference in the results we achieved.

Role of Parents: Any plan to improve education needs to incorporate parents. Many parents are frustrated because they believe school teachers should be more qualified and capable than they are. A good role model is Sonya Carson, the mother of Dr. Ben Carson, a candidate during the 2016 presidential primary. Regardless of your political affiliation, it's difficult to ignore the influence Sonya Carson had on her two young boys as you'll see in Dr. Carson's story.[34] It's full of hope and possibility.

The best way to improve our education system involves joint responsibility among parents, teachers, students, the school support crew, and the community. Here are other important issues under the Education pillar:

- ✦ Points or Knowledge? I'm concerned about the vision for education being short-sighted. It appears students and sometimes parents fight for points toward a grade but they don't fight for knowledge. Frequently, students (and parents) claimed they "deserved" a better grade, but I haven't yet had students (or parents) claim they were cheated out of the knowledge expected. We have to turn this attitude around.

- ✦ Should Everyone Go to College? In my opinion, no. College can be a growth experience, but many students currently enrolled in colleges have no desire to be there. Without sincere desire, their talents are better directed toward other challenges.

✦ Creative Destruction. "The only constant is change."
This refers to helping people recognize the need to
keep learning so they stay employable. Are we incen-
tivizing them appropriately? Do they understand the
consequences if they don't stay employed?

Fortunately, the skill I continue to hone—leader
development—is indestructible. As long as we have
people who are scripted as much by emotion as logic,
we'll need people to lead them. Even so, I spend at
least a quarter of my workweek on my personal education to stay up with the latest advancements. In the
last decade, I've gained knowledge in subjects such
as the DiSC profile, Emotional Intelligence, and Dr.
Clifton's Strengths Finder process, as well as others.

✦ *The World of Technology.* In the future, the definition
of haves/have-nots will be determined by one's
degree of skill using technology. That means always
keeping ourselves in the know.

✦ *Gaming: Bane or Boon?* There's an incredible advantage
to using game technology in both the workplace and
the education systems. Simply put, if young people
gravitate toward games, why not use that to *everyone's*
advantage by incorporating gaming techniques and
technology into our systems and structures?

The purpose of education is Unlocking, Engaging, and Optimizing human potential. It's based on the belief that each person
has something grand to contribute, so let's make sure all our efforts in this realm do exactly that. If we work together to modernize the U.S. educational system, it can again serve as a model for
others around the world.

If you have ideas that might help, please share them so we can provide the Lift that's vital to making progress.

Energy

At some point, society will advance to using only natural and renewable energy resources. Even without harnessing the power of the sun, the earth generates significant energy. For example, when we're capable of capturing and harnessing the energy in thunderstorms, we'll not likely need any other sources to fully meet our needs. Someday I hope this becomes one of our collective "Moon Shots."

The parameters are vital: We need energy that's abundant, reliable (not only in the production but in the distribution), cost-effective (relatively inexpensive and efficient), and as clean and safe as possible given our current beliefs/technology.

To help people be positive and productive, at KiVisions we say: *Learn from yesterday, Look to tomorrow, but be Successful today.* Combined with our Left Hand, Right Hand concept, that's powerful. Bottom line: We need to be realistic. For the foreseeable future, we have to rely on fossil fuels to meet our needs. Although I'm not interested in returning to the Fred Flintstone days, that's where we'd find ourselves if we eliminate fossil fuels due to the paltry contribution of current renewable options. Either we use fossil fuels or we take a giant leap and accept massive use of nuclear energy until (likely decades from now) we master the technology that can relegate fossil fuels to history.

As energy alternatives, I hope scientists explore all possible sources: solar, hydrogen, biofuels, wind (as long as we aren't slicing and dicing our feathered friends at alarming rates), and other natural possibilities.

The Matter of Consistency: This energy concern affects at least two pillars—Energy and Health. Is man's use of carbon-based fuels negatively affecting the earth's environment? This question offers an opportunity to discuss a significant leadership issue: consistency. On Net, we want to leave the world a better place for our kids/grandkids and we're willing to take reasonable steps to do so.

Numerous reports provide an answer to this "carbon impact" issue, but they're often diametrically opposed to one another. I sought factors that can help me rate the respective reports relative to the potential bias, track record, and personal actions of the authors.

Given the research, I understand why many are not persuaded to change their behaviors. Many who claim carbon-based fuels have caused climate change say we must take drastic measures to save the planet, but they haven't changed *their* behaviors. For example, the city of Davos, Switzerland, hosts the World Economic Forum (WEF), an annual meeting of global political and business elites (often referred to simply as Davos). A recent conference addressed today's global climate situation. However, instead of consolidating their trips, many of the attendees flew in on their own fossil-fuel-burning private jets.[35] How does that square with what they're telling others to do? This is a leadership issue of massive proportions.

Any leadership offered in a "Do as I say, not as I do" manner will never be respected. Once this behavior is discovered, it's not likely these "leaders" will secure many followers—for this issue and all issues. True Leaders model the behavior they desire in others, even if they must take somewhat "painful" actions to be true to their beliefs.

"The grid" is responsible for distributing the energy desperately needed, and the grid through the U.S. is old and fragile. This serious issue only started to get the public's attention in 2016. Be prepared to hear proposals on additional infrastructure projects to both modernize and harden our grid.

Harden? You may have heard the initials EMP (Electro-Magnetic Pulse), referring to a potential concern with the grid. This is becoming an all-too-real threat or possibility. In the "old days," it was assumed a nuclear armed enemy would have to unleash hell on most of our major cities and military complexes to defeat us. In theory, that's no longer the case. Experts warn that the EMP created by even one nuclear warhead detonated in the atmosphere over a strategic location in the United States would cause massive disruption to our power sources.[36] We rely so extensively on these sources that some claim we'd experience greater than 50 percent casualties among the U.S. population within the first year. "Hardening" our grid (taking the measures necessary to protect it from an EMP) sounds like an issue for True Leaders to deal with appropriately—and immediately.

Governance

Governance requires us to re-engage as a way to ensure we're On Course. At all levels, governance must have strict oversight—not only elected bodies but all bodies that make collective decisions affecting opportunities to Unlock, Engage, and Optimize our potential. When I make this statement, people (usually accompanied by a furrowed brow) ask, "Wait a minute—aren't our governance bodies supposed to provide oversight to other activities?" To this I respond, "Yeah . . . and how's that working?"

Let's cite these financial issues at the federal level to confirm this concern: huge deficits, astronomical debt, and unfunded liabilities that boggle the mind. These can "cripple" future economies. Our children and grandchildren will inherit the responsibility to fix the mess older generations (mine included) have created/allowed. The fix won't be easy, but it will only get worse if we don't take care of it soon. Plus, only a few indisputable issues are cited here; many more are causing us to get Off Course.

What needs to change? We need to make better decisions and lead from *where we are* to *where we should be*. Many have accepted this responsibility, but more good people have to take their place on governing bodies. Governing bodies—from the federal government to the UN and the local school board—have huge scope, scale, and effect. They influence all aspects of the Foundation: Unifying Vision, Health, Energy, and Education.

Let's encourage our governing bodies to provide Lift while not inducing Drag or, in the worst case, Dead Weight. Lift means to help our dynamos of success—individuals and the businesses they start—create opportunities for others through good jobs.

Politicians: These "government servants" are well compensated, so why do vast numbers of people believe our politicians have failed to achieve the results we expect? Perhaps one answer is *falsitude*—the false attitude of those who believe that because of their position, they're experts in any field they choose. There's even a term for people who give advice outside the area of their expertise: *ultracrepidarian*. (Try building that into a discussion at your next party!)

Too many decisions are made based on what "feels right" rather than what works.

When was the last time you chose a candidate based on a bumper sticker you saw? Almost as bad, who would count the number of bumper stickers they see for their candidate to affirm their choice? Instead of using bumper stickers for validation, let's commit to investigating the elected officials who can have a huge effect on our lives.

Musician Pete Townshend and his band The Who wrote the song "We Won't Get Fooled Again." It's become a mantra after someone who gets into office proves to be merely another phony politician. Yet, what makes us believe we won't get fooled again? The same people using the bumper sticker affirmation. When their initial pain subsides, they fall back into old habits and get fooled repeatedly.

One reason people get fooled is the Sports Team Mindset mentioned earlier. We need to carefully monitor people who we think have the same values as we do. If it's assumed the letter a politician lists after his/her name (e.g., D for Democrat or R for Republican) implies a constancy of values, we're doomed to be fooled again and again.

Because the complexity of the issues is so vast, I don't claim to have "the" solution. However, I'd only be part of the problem if I didn't offer ideas on how we might improve our federal governance issues. (See Appendix E for these thoughts.)

World Affairs: Not all issues requiring oversight are concentrated at home, of course. Getting interested in world affairs focuses you on issues of peace, freedom, and prosperity around the world, including:

+ trade

+ human rights (determination and enforcement of acceptable behavior standards through our diplomatic corps and military)

A Proactive Approach: RAVOlUtion

Because our Foundation is in trouble, even crumbling, it's time to take off the blinders and apply a proactive approach. My solution: a RAVOlUtion.

Most uprisings are fueled by anger and fear, using violence as a primary tool. The RAVOlUtion is intended to appeal to everything that's good in people and be the nonviolent, peaceful solution we can enact before it's too late. We can have a wondrous future if we each commit to the tenets of the RAVOlUtion and help others do the same. Let's review these tenets again as noted under Leader Qualities in Chapter 3.

+ **R**esponsibility: When the U.S. Constitution was drafted, the Bill of Rights was necessary to ensure "We the People" maintained our rights to life, liberty, and the pursuit of happiness. The incredible prosperity that's materialized now requires we become Masters of Success. We've made quantum leaps in technology, which has helped us reap untold wealth throughout our economic spectrum. However, the human psyche has not made similar advancements. Many of the problems are due to a focus on the Scarcity Mentality, time-wasting distractions, and a lack of focus on pursuing our purpose. To change that, let's supplement the Bill of Rights with a Bill of Responsibilities, with the hope that every able-bodied, able-minded person will contribute. Joe Tye of Values Coach, Inc. has crafted a Bill of Responsibilities[37] worth exploring. (See Appendix F.)

Let's start by accepting we have two key parts to play. First, our purpose: Do everything you can to Unlock, Engage, and Optimize your potential to bring that purpose to fruition. Second, accept a secondary responsibility to engage in the Foundation for Success.

+ **A**ccountability: There are no perfect humans; many have great intentions, but as Marshall Goldsmith outlined in his book *What Got You Here Won't Get You There* (see Appendix D), leader development requires someone who will hold your feet to the fire. You need a mechanism to ensure your day-to-day activities don't distract you from achieving your purpose.

✦ **V**alue the Potential in Humans: Dr. Covey taught me the most mature form of interaction between humans is interdependence. When we recognize the importance of allowing all humans to contribute, many of our social ills will be markedly reduced, maybe even eliminated.

✦ **O**wnership: True Leaders understand that one way to Unlock, Engage, and Optimize (UEO) human potential is to give the people you lead "ownership" of various processes, resources, and more. From the RAVOlUtion perspective, we recognize that to live in the most civil society possible means each person takes ownership of the process leading to a desired outcome. Only then can change for the better become the norm.

✦ **U**nifying Vision: This is the first element in the Foundation and a key element of the RAVOlUtion. Let's craft a viable vision and enjoy the fruits of this powerful tool.

Join me in the RAVOlUtion to re-ignite that fire in the belly. Ensure your contributions result in top-notch outcomes and spread the word about the need to re-engage.

Need to Re-Engage

Join me in the RAVOlUtion to re-ignite that fire in the belly while ensuring your primary and secondary contributions result in top-notch outcomes. Spread the word to help others realize the need to re-engage. Let's do so before the ability to achieve our dream becomes another relic of history.

Collectively, the RAVOlUtion can build a groundswell of support. As your wingman, I explore this topic and share the thoughts and successes of others in various forums. Instead of being angry, let's take the steps that will get us back On Course.

SETTING THE STAGE FOR YOUR FUTURE

W hat happens from here?

One of my strongest beliefs is that people have more potential than anyone can fathom. That belief has ignited a flame in me to help Unlock, Engage, and Optimize that potential—including *your* potential. It's my purpose, my dream, to help people find the course toward a better future for us all.

To do that, I've developed tools and insights to help you better use the Successful Ventures in Human Dynamics Model. Key points are:

1. Recognize there's nothing easy about leading people, but the Model makes it much easier.

2. Point the "plane" toward the desired destination.

3. Work to achieve the Vision:

✦ Ensure the "plane" is properly "outfitted" to accomplish the mission/achieve the vision.

✦ Balance the four forces. Optimum advantage usually entails increasing Lift and Thrust while decreasing Drag and Weight.

✦ Once you "take off," avoid the "storms" and effectively deal with those conditions outside your control.

Turning Turbulence into Opportunity

No preparation ensures a smooth ride. When I started flying, I felt nervous whenever we hit the slightest turbulence, but my instructor never did. When I hit turbulence after trading my flight suit for a business suit, I wondered if I had anything worth contributing. It was an incredibly demoralizing period—*but* had I not gone through it, I wouldn't be helping good people become Great Leaders today.

In fact, after I became more comfortable, a favorite thing became enjoying the turbulence while "riding" the tops of cumulus clouds. Figuratively, "riding the tops of the clouds" lets you know you have things to work on while becoming a True Leader, but these will also help you become a Great Leader.

---

4. Incorporate the 5 Prime Values of a True Leader to ensure you start out On Course.

5. In addition to your primary role, accept a secondary role to increase Lift in the Foundation for Success.

What role will you play? Society over time has built technological marvels that have improved the standard of living for many. Now, let's progress in how we think about and work with others. You and I can improve the standard of living for many, including ourselves.

The Helping True Leaders Soar to Greatness series will continue to address a host of topics, such as Flight Controls (to help you maneuver and get where you want to go), Navigation (to help ensure you stay On Course), Dealing with Emergencies, and more to help good people become Great Leaders.

Together, we can rekindle the American Dream and be able to say "yes" to each of the 5 Key Questions. Be part of the RAVOlUtion. Let's serve as role models for others around the world.

We can help people realize the benefits of Lifting their societies out of poverty. Let's heal that which divides us; let's preserve freedom and keep us safe from threats to our health and way of life; let's keep us on a bright path to greater prosperity; let's work so that we're proud to sign our names to everything we produce and the services we provide. By doing so, we'll be fulfilled and can Soar to our preferred future!

To eventually achieve fulfillment, incorporate these steps into your plan:

1. Become an ACE.

2. Commit to/become a True Leader.

3. Walk the path toward becoming a Great Leader.

Making a Difference

For me, success is knowing I've made a difference. It can be personal and sometimes highly emotional as the following examples show.

One of my treasured memories comes from a request by my dad who served in the U.S. Marines during World War II. Unlike my grandpa who told me every World War I story he remembered, Dad shared very little, but I knew he became a brother-in-arms to many. He was assigned as a gunner aboard the U.S.S. Hancock (an aircraft carrier assigned to the Pacific). His job consisted of ensuring Japanese planes did as little damage to the ship as possible. I know he had a particular dislike for the Kamikaze missions.

After the war, members of Dad's Marine platoon did their best to stay in touch by holding frequent reunions. They shared the responsibility for hosting the reunions and a few years back—decades after the war—it was Dad's turn to host. He asked me to be the guest speaker at their main dinner. I was honored and wanted to make sure I did what I could to make the occasion memorable.

Now, if you haven't served in the military, it may be difficult to understand the chain of command and separation that often occurs between "the men" and the officers, commonly referred to as "the brass." Dad's Marine platoon was composed of "the men." Having friends in the right places, I was able to secure a letter of thanks to the platoon members for their dignified service and sacrifices endured as a result of their commitment to the country during the war. Lots of people who served in the military wonder if anybody cares about the sacrifices they made for others. From the response of Dad's platoon to the letter from the Commandant of the Marine Corps (the highest ranking Marine and a member of the Joint Chiefs of Staff), I knew they clearly appreciated this long overdue recognition they deserved. Indeed, I didn't realize *one letter of recognition* could have such a powerful effect. It's a great lesson for anyone who desires to be a good leader.

Then I thought back to a letter I'd received years before. At times when I doubt the difference I've made in this world, I refer to it.

October 1988

Major, I just wanted to express my sentiments to you personally.

First, you have been a great inspiration to me and my career. You have taught me a great deal since your arrival at Pease Air Force Base. Your leadership qualities are above anyone that I have ever known. You have made my career in the United States Air Force a very memorable one. You have taught me what it means to be a member of the USAF and the responsibilities that go along with being an American fighting man. I have told you in the past that YOU are what keeps me going, wanting to stick with it and wanting to spend my life defending this great country of ours.

You have meant as much to me as my own father!! I have grown up a tremendous amount and taken on a lot of responsibilities that otherwise might not have come my way, because of you. Sir, not only have you taught me about the Air Force but, also, about life and how to deal with and treat other people with respect. I certainly respect you, what you stand for, and how to become a Great Leader to other people. As you may remember, my speech at the Professional Military Education graduation was on professionalism; it was based on what you have taught ME. Not only have you been a Great Leader but a great friend!

Sir, I wish you the best of luck at your next assignment. I also hope that someday our paths may cross again. I will truly miss you, your leadership, and your friendship. But, I will NEVER forget you and what I have learned from you. I will serve this country as a good NCO as I have learned from you. Take good care of yourself and your family. May we meet again sometime in the future.

Yours sincerely,

Jack M_____

I get emotional every time I look at this letter—to think I had this kind of influence on another person. I can only dream of the impact Jack has had on others since that time. This, more than anything else, taught me I was on the right track. Within six short years from the days I was having sleepless nights, I was able to make a real difference. It helped me realize how comfortable I am with KiVisions' definition of a leader: *One who shows the way.*

My recommendation to you: *Show the way.*

Knowing I've made a positive difference in many lives helps me keep my Heading Indicator pointing North.

To What Will You Give Your Life?

After one of his magnificent concerts, world-renowned pianist Van Cliburn was approached by an admirer who'd been in the audience. The emotional fan grasped Cliburn's hand and said, "I would give my life to be able to play the piano like that."

The pianist smiled and replied, "I did . . ."

It's your time to take the controls and soar! Use the Successful Ventures in Human Dynamics Model and start out On Course.

We can still achieve a better tomorrow by committing to unlocking, engaging, and optimizing our unique potential. Will you help make it happen? Will you commit your life to changing the world?

True Leaders accept responsibility for making a positive difference in their world. Together, we can increase peace, freedom, and prosperity for all.

AFTERWORD

have known Ken Pasch on a professional, educational, and personnel level for over 25 years. Early in our relationship, I recognized his unique skill in understanding—at all levels—the complex differences between leadership and management. Over the years, as his military, business, academic, and personnel experience broadened, his knowledge, understanding, and application of leadership became even more focused.

Through his career, Ken has focused on what he considers one of the most critical factors for success in any endeavor in life—leadership. *On Course,* Ken's approach to leadership, is referred to as the Successful Ventures in Human Dynamics Model.

The Successful Ventures in Human Dynamics Model came from an epiphany born out of frustration when he shifted from flying in the U.S. Air Force to leadership and management positions at medical centers. He knew his leadership "style" wasn't working. During one of many sleepless nights, he wondered about the similarities of getting both an aircraft and an organization off the ground. Applying this thought, he found success! From that, his life's purpose formed: To help prevent others from experiencing similar pain and frustration while giving them tools to *unlock, engage, and optimize their own potential and the potential in those they lead.*

Thus this book provides the Flight Plan for Helping Good People Become Great Leaders at the individual and organizational level. This is also the mission of Ken's company, KiVisions.

He knows this life-changing model isn't a quick fix; it takes time and demands a concerted effort. In the process, it encourages and challenges you to "take up the mantle" of transformation, and then break down myths that plague our world. Ken believes that you—individually and collectively—can play a significant role in helping society achieve greater peace, freedom, and prosperity.

Ken's life experiences have prepared him to mentor you to follow the Successful Ventures in Human Dynamics Model. If you do, you will emerge as a Great Leader, achieve fulfillment, and be successful both professionally and personally.

—Colonel (retired) Raymond J. Chappelle, USAF, MSC

ACKNOWLEDGMENTS

First, I would like to acknowledge those who helped me get my start. The list is long so I will pare it down to my primary influences: my mom Lois, my dad Ken, Grandma Donato, and Grandpa Donato on my mom's side. (On my dad's side, I had a great relationship with my Grandpa Herb, which was more fun than formative. Unfortunately, my dad's mom passed before I was born.)

Grandma Donato was a truly loving and caring woman, and Grandpa Donato was a great teacher. He taught me to be quiet and gentle enough to allow squirrels to climb onto my shoulder so I could feed them. That takes a special touch, and he had it.

Mom and Dad were tough on me and my siblings. I didn't appreciate this when I was a kid, but I wouldn't be where I am now without their direction.

I'm now able to help good people become Great Leaders because of those who helped me Unlock, Engage, and Optimize my potential as I grew up. Thanks to you all!

Each book of the series will acknowledge the long list of people who have and continue to help me. Here, I want to thank my editor, Barbara McNichol. Her patience and tutelage has been vital in helping me craft the material on these pages. If she had been my composition teacher in high school, I'd be much further along than I am today.

I also thank David Hancock of Morgan James for being open, honest, and willing to develop a process that mutually supports his publishing business and the author.

Finally, I want to thank Terry Whalin, Acquisitions Editor at Morgan James. He managed the project as though it was submitted by John Grisham.

ABOUT THE AUTHOR

Ken Pasch's dream: Help good people become great leaders and achieve fulfillment.

On Course represents Phase 1 of Ken's 9-Phase Helping True Leaders Soar to Greatness leader development series. It features the KiVisions Leader Development Process that includes the revolutionary Successful Ventures in Human Dynamics Model Ken created.

This Model came from an epiphany born out of frustration when Ken transitioned from flying in the U.S. Air Force to leading medical centers. He knew his leadership "style" wasn't working. During one of many sleepless nights, he wondered about the similarities of getting both an aircraft and an organization off the ground. His approach found success! From that, his life's purpose formed: *To help prevent others from experiencing similar pain and frustration while giving them tools to unlock, engage, and optimize their own potential and the potential in those they lead.*

Ken's broad experience includes working with the U.S. military and also with associations such as the American College of Healthcare Executives, global corporations such as Johnson & Johnson, and educational institutions such as the Smeal College of Business at Penn State University.

Ken loves spending time with his family enjoying the beauty of this earth. One day, he hopes to break the record for the biggest trout caught in Pennsylvania!

You can follow Ken's blog at www.KiVisions.com and email him at KiVisions@KiVisions.com

APPENDICES

Appendix A: The KiVisions Leader Development Process

The KiVisions Leader Development Process

To Help Good People Become Great Leaders (i.e., Unlock, Engage, and Optimize the potential in those they lead) and Soar (i.e., achieve/exceed personal, professional, and organizational goals). The KiVisions Leader Development Process provides a Model all True Leaders can use, a System engineered to help those leaders effectively use the Model, and a Challenge to keep those leaders motivated for the long journey to become a Great Leader.

The Successful Ventures in Human Dynamics Model ™

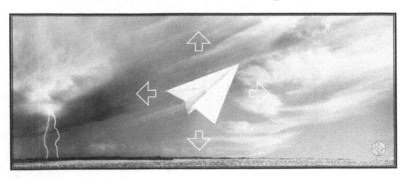

The Model recognizes that what it takes to get an aircraft or an organization "off the ground and to its destination" are amazingly similar. The plane in the Model represents a number of possible focal points including you, your "crew", organization, etc. The "paper airplane" is intended to help you realize the Model works for all leaders. Regardless of the size or type of organization, the factors and dynamic motion are the same. The differences are in the scale and scope of the operations. Now, a brief look at each Step in the Model:

1. The plane must be pointed toward the desired destination and

2. Properly "outfitted" to accomplish the mission/ achieve the vision.

   (Understanding the impact and effectively using the 4 "forces" below will help you become a better leader. The key: As a leader, you must balance these forces to ensure the organization achieves its goals. No force is necessarily positive, no force is necessarily negative.)

3. *Lift* (represented by the up arrow) gives you the *potential* to "get off the ground". Lift is primarily created by those things that inspire each person to derive the motivation to achieve the organization's vision & mission. The caveat: If you aren't careful, you might "go too high". The higher you go requires greater mastery and might cause you to lose perspective.

4. *Thrust* (represented by the arrow facing right) propels you forward and allows *potential* Lift to become *actual* Lift. Thrust is primarily created by coordinated efforts (by you, your "crew", &/or groups) that produce effective results. The caveat: If you aren't careful, you might "go too fast".

5. *Drag* (represented by the arrow facing left), primarily caused by ineffectiveness, holds you back. The caveat: Being "held back" can be a good thing. Most organizations need at least one "Devil's Advocate" to ensure careful consideration of what/when/how/why/where things are being done.

6. *Weight* (represented by the down arrow) makes it harder to "get off the ground and climb". All Weight is inevitably affected by "gravity", an External Condition that will be dealt with in our books. Dead-Weight, potential that remains "locked up" in humans, is the key issue leaders must solve. It indicates a lack of a clear vision & mission or the "crew's" connection to both. The caveat: As the saying goes, being "grounded in reality" can be a good thing.

As a leader, you have some measure of control, or at least influence, over the 6 Steps above. To be a complete leader, you must also be prepared to navigate through those things outside your control.

7. *External Conditions* (represented by the storm and the wind "pushing" the clouds) are factors and issues over which you likely have little, if any, control or influence.

   a. Some External Conditions are obstacles that should be *avoided*. The storm depicted in the Model is a natural obstacle and dangerous to fly through. Organizations experience many "storms"; learn how and then take steps to avoid them. Many of these storms will be specific to your organization or industry.

   b. Other External Conditions cannot be avoided; *you need to deal with them*. For flyers, wind is unavoidable; not only is it always present, the direction and velocity frequently change; it affects take-off, navigation, etc. Laws and regulations are examples you might encounter. All unavoidable issues will likely impact your organizational plans and outcomes to some extent, great or small.

Although the Model has potentially broader implications, we will focus on the decisions made by the leaders of an organization that relate to people, systems, structures, etc.

Next, the System that will help you best use the Model.

The Gyroscope System™

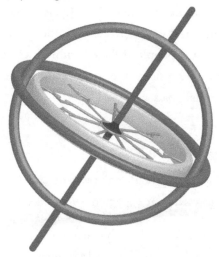

The components of *The Gyroscope System* include:

The "brands" that support The KiVisions Leader Development Process:

1. ***Soaring Leaders Academy™:*** Our teaching/mentoring "brand" educates and clarifies concepts for leaders who are hungry to Grow Forward™. Scope: Individual &/or "crew" growth. Focus: Build awareness of and provide "how to" knowledge in the skills necessary to become a Great Leader.

2. ***True Leaders Forum™:*** Our coaching and facilitated-mastermind-groups "brand" helps leaders establish and achieve their personalized vision. Scope: Individual & "crew" growth. Focus: Build awareness of an individual's current capability and provide the opportunity to improve the skills necessary to become a Great Leader.

3. ***Impact on Results™:*** Our consulting "brand" is based upon our proprietary C.P.E.G.=+I.O.R.™ method. Scope: Organizational performance and growth. Focus: Ensure the people affiliated with our client organizations and the systems they use are aligned to achieve organizational goals.

Our Levels of Leader Readiness

Recognizing leader development can't be "one-size-fits-all", our programs are geared toward your expected level of leader readiness:

1. ***Emerging Leaders:*** relatively inexperienced leaders who are learning to understand/deal with expectations.

2. ***Leaders with History:*** these leaders have gained depth and breadth of experience and are learning to consistently achieve excellence.

3. ***Leaders of Leaders:*** these leaders have advanced to the level where they understand the necessity and are diligently attempting to master the development of other leaders to ensure the sustainability of the organization.

Imbedded within the *Gyroscope System* is our ultimate *Challenge to Leaders:* Earn the Ratings that will ensure you have the ability and confidence to serve as a Great Leader and navigate evermore complex situations. In addition, we offer 2 Complements that supplement the Ratings to ensure you have the skills and tools you need. Shown in recommended order of completion:

1. *Ground School:* the Foundational Complement that provides a framework for effective leader growth and development; it is necessary to ensure leaders at all levels start out On Course.

2. Rating #1: *Earn Your Wings*^{TM}: Oriented toward helping "Emerging Leaders" fully grasp the importance of managing expectations; plus, it gives more senior leaders a baseline for developing Emerging Leaders.

3. Rating #2: *Master Flight*^{TM}: Oriented toward helping "Leaders with History" consistently achieve excellence; plus, it gives more senior leaders a baseline for developing Leaders with History.

4. Rating #3: *Soar*^{TM}: Oriented toward developing "Leaders of Leaders"; it is the pinnacle rating for Great Leaders wishing to achieve and sustain exceptional results through the development of other leaders; it also serves as an extraordinary succession planning primer.

5. *Maintain Currency:* This Complement supplements each Rating by helping ensure leaders maintain a path toward greater competency within the Rating they have earned.

"Helping True Leaders Soar to Greatness" leader development series.

Each Phase of the series was built to unlock the secrets of *The Successful Ventures in Human Dynamics Model* and support one of the Ratings/Complements in the *Challenge to Leaders*. However, although you will likely limit your growth and the results you might enjoy, it is not a requirement that you accept the Challenge. Some of our customers initially gain great insight from one or more Phases in the series and then decide to see just how high they can soar through the Challenge. Here are the Phases in the series and the Rating/Complement each supports:

To support *Ground School:*

✦ Phase-1: "On Course: Become a Great Leader & Soar!"™

To support Rating #1: *Earn Your Wings:*

✦ Phase-2: "Become the Boss *You* Always Wanted"™

✦ Phase-3: "The Leader's Magic Mirror"™ (2 parts):

+ First Look: Your Internal RE.F.L.E.C.T.I.O.N.™

+ Second Take: Your External I.M.A.G.E.™

✦ Phase-4: "Lead with P.R.I.D.E."™

To support Rating #2: *Master Flight:*

✦ Phase-5: "True Leaders Grow Forward"™

✦ Phase-6: "The Leader's Path: From the Ideal, through the Ordeal, to the Real Deal"™

✦ Phase-7: "The Leader's 'Investment' Tool: Ken's I.R.A."™

To support Rating #3: *Soar:*

✦ Phase-8: "Make Your Organization C.L.I.C.K."™

To support *Maintain Currency:*

✦ Phase-9: _____ (Built to meet your needs and keep you Growing Forward)

(A video that explains how our Gyroscope System incorporates the components outlined above can be viewed on our website:

www.KiVisions.com/WorkWithUs)

Appendix B: Table of Qualities and Clarifying Questions for Leader Categories

Qualities and Clarifying Questions	True Leader	Wanna-Be Leader	False Leader
What's the person's value set?	Consistent Abundance Mentality; has adopted and tries to live by the 5 Prime Values	Inconsistent; no clear sense of values	Consistent Scarcity Mentality; has not adopted the 5 Prime Values; likely doesn't love him/herself
How does the person handle rewards?	Shares rewards with those responsible for the achievement(s)	If required, will share rewards but only to maintain his/her position, perks, and power	Keeps rewards for him/herself but often doles out tidbits to keep people dependent on him/her
Does the person share credit for a job well done (offshoot of rewards)?	Shares in proportional measures	Might share credit, but there's no rhyme or reason to his/her methodology	At worst, believes others have little to do with victories
What's the person's intent for those s/he leads?	Help others grow to become self-sufficient, fulfilled	Get others to realize how great s/he is; many need to be worshiped by followers, defined as those who work for (not with) him/her; at minimum, expects others to adore him/her	Keep those working for him/her (and often any others affiliated) subservient and dependent on him/her

Qualities and Clarifying Questions	True Leader	Wanna-Be Leader	False Leader
Is the person's vision unifying?	Yes. True Leaders earnestly pursue their purpose with passion and help others see the value in doing the same.	Proposed vision often sounds good and it might serve the group (coincidentally). S/he has good intentions but lacks the ability or work ethic to develop a vision that truly serves the group.	Proposed vision often sounds good, urgent, even necessary, and is conveyed with emotion, which is necessary to stir up negative inclinations.
Whom does it serve?	Serves/unifies the group	Not well delineated so it's hard to tell whom it serves	Usually divisive and serves the False Leader only
What's the clarity of the vision the person proposes?	Clear	Fuzzy or disjointed	Shrouded, although it may appear to be clear
What is the person's vision directed toward?	Accomplishing a higher purpose for the group	Ensuring the person's own aggrandizement	Accomplishing a purpose that serves his/her ultimate, often nefarious, goal
What are the proposed outcomes of the person's vision?	Often, increased peace, freedom, and prosperity	Usually fuzzy	Self-serving and divisive to keep power in his/her hands

Qualities and Clarifying Questions	True Leader	Wanna-Be Leader	False Leader
What's the likely effect of enacting his/her vision?	On Course	Off Course	Wrong Course
How well does the person take responsibility for keeping the group's focus on the vision?	Laser-like focus on priorities; gains credibility by being willing to join in on the necessary "dirty" work	Distracted; often wastes own and others' time on issues that have no bearing on the vision	Maintains focus on the self-serving vision and won't tolerate those who don't buy in
What type of work ethic does the person employ?	Focuses on productivity but knows when it's time for a break to avoid burnout (an area for improvement for most True Leaders)	Often appears to be working hard but gets distracted. Followers frequently say, "We were spinning our wheels and getting nowhere."	Often expects unreasonable output due to lack of the 5 Prime Values. Followers believe they're owed more than they get but are afraid to ask the False Leader who fills their needs at others' expense.
How well does the person strive to improve, especially the skill of leadership?	Continuously, not realizing how good they are, which drives them to seek even more knowledge and ability	Often assumes having a big Rolodex filled with business cards of movers and shakers suffices for the work of continuous improvement	Often strives for more control rather than more capability

Qualities and Clarifying Questions	True Leader	Wanna-Be Leader	False Leader
Does the person accept accountability?	May seem harsh as they're usually intolerant of those unwilling to fulfill their part in the organization's mission; willingly listen to cogent arguments that differ from the expected path	Shows little true accountability; often issues ultimatums but doesn't follow through	Intolerant of those unable, unprepared, or unwilling to achieve his/her mission
Is the person willing to admit a mistake?	If it serves the group, will do so willingly but isn't a saint!	Not likely if it will tarnish his/her image; instead, looks for someone else to take the blame or redirect attention	If it serves the False leader, will do so carefully; otherwise, crucifies a scapegoat and ensures the story indicates the scapegoat as perpetrator
When times get tough, does the person stand up for what s/he believes?	Yes. Will likely take the blame for things gone wrong even if s/he had little direct control over the outcome; strongly believes in sharing authority but maintaining ultimate accountability	Not likely because what s/he most seems to believe in is him/herself, not principles	Will stubbornly stick to his/her plans even if they're ill conceived (e.g., Hitler); when things don't go as planned, will look for others to blame

Qualities and Clarifying Questions	True Leader	Wanna-Be Leader	False Leader
Does the person value human potential?	Strongly believes that's why others are on the crew	Hasn't sorted out the role others play; often, hasn't considered deeply why others are on the crew	Sees others as pawns in his/her grand scheme; can be "nut jobs" with few if any values
How does the person distribute ownership?	Meticulously ensures proper ownership is bestowed upon those who have responsibility for various processes and resources	Usually not comfortable releasing control over processes or resources; thus, people do what they must but little more	Easily bestows ownership on others— when things go wrong!

Appendix C: Glossary of Terms

Abundance Mentality (the short version): Taking a "We Win" approach toward others with whom we work, with at least equal focus on WCIC and WIFM (see definitions under W).

ACE: Live with an Abundance Mentality, Concentrate on Priorities, and Earnestly Pursue your Purpose . . . with Passion! It's the approach good people take as they work toward becoming a True Leader.

Ahead of the Curve: Represents a statistical placement on a bell curve; at minimum, work to ensure you are at the top of the curve or right of the midpoint.

CLdrC: Certified Leader Coach. To earn this designation requires a thorough understanding of the KiVisions Leader Development Process and a proven ability to relate the concepts within that process through teaching, mentoring, coaching, and consulting.

CPEG = +IOR: A proprietary consulting method based on: Communication yields Productivity, Engagement yields Growth; combined, they yield a positive Impact On Results.

Crew: Replaces the term "team" because of the KiVisions Leader Development Process's connection to flying.

False Leaders (short version): Dangerous leaders out for themselves.

Falsitude: Refers to a false attitude of those who believe that, because they're a relative expert in one field, they're naturally an expert in any other field they choose.

Fly-by Scootings: Actions of Would-Be leaders who believe leading means ensuring people in their organization see their faces once in a while.

Gyroscope System: A tool and visual representation used by the staff at KiVisions to help True Leaders learn the Successful Ventures in Human Dynamics Model.

Mission: (short version) A written description of what the organization does to achieve the Vision.

People in POA: People in Positions of Authority.

Power curve: Below a certain airspeed, maintaining that speed counter-intuitively requires more Thrust rather than less Thrust. The consequences of being "behind the curve" can be disastrous. In this situation, the primary forces to balance are Lift, Thrust, and Drag.

Pushing the envelope: A set of performance limits that may not be safely exceeded. To "push the envelope" implies you're searching for your actual limits.

Scarcity Mentality (short version): Taking an "I Win" approach toward others with whom you work, likely with greater focus on WIFM than WCIC (see definitions under W).

Sports Team Mindset: The idea that, when debating with others, one's team (sports, politics, religion, etc.) is always right, even when it's obviously wrong. This mentality often causes people to believe any means to an end is acceptable.

True Leaders (short version): Leaders who empower their crews and act as role models.

True Leaders Code: "I will be *dauntless*. I will do what needs to be done, by when it needs to be done, in a manner consistent with my values, especially on days I don't feel up to it. Many people are counting on me to fulfill my calling, my purpose, my mission."

UEO: Unlock, Engage, and Optimize (always referring to human potential).

Successful Ventures in Human Dynamics Model: A model True Leaders can use to become Great Leaders.

Vision: A written description of where you (if personal) or your organization wants to go and what you want to be.

Wanna-Be Leaders (short version): Disingenuous and distracted leaders.

WCIC: What Can I Contribute?

WIFM: What's In it For Me?

Wingman: The position given only to the person with whom flyers entrust their lives. (The term has been embezzled by those with more prurient interests.) In the true nature of the term, a KiVisions' Wingman is available to be with you as you earn all three ratings and Soar, not score. In this Model, a Wingman serves as a coach, mentor, champion, confidant, and resource.

Would-Be Leaders: Refers to people with characteristics of both Wanna-Be and False Leaders.

Appendix D: On Course Library

Brown, Paul. *Own Your Future*. American Management Association (AMACOM), 2014.

Christensen, Clayton, Curtis W. Johnson, and Michael B. Horn. *Disrupting Class: How Disruptive Innovation Will Change the Way the World Learns*. McGraw-Hill, 2011.

Collins, James C. and Jerry I. Porras. *Built to Last*. HarperCollins, 2004.

Covey, Stephen R. *The 7 Habits of Highly Effective People*. Simon & Schuster, 1989.

Davis, Burke. *Marine! The Life of Chesty Puller*. Open Road Media, 1962.

Frankl, Victor. *Man's Search for Meaning*. Beacon Press, 1963.

Gladwell, Malcom. *Blink*. Back Bay Books, 2007.

Godin, Seth. *The Icarus Deception: How High Will You Fly?* Portfolio/Penguin, 2012.

Goldsmith, Marshall and Mark Reiter. *What Got You Here Won't Get You There*. Hatchett Books, 2007.

Grove, Andrew S. *High Output Management*. Vintage, 1995.

Lencioni, Patrick. *5 Dysfunctions of a Team*. Jossey-Bass, 2002.

Lencioni, Patrick. *Death by Meeting: A Leadership Fable...About Solving the Most Painful Problem in Business*. Jossey-Bass, 2004.

McGonigal, Jane. *Reality Is Broken*. Penguin Press, 2011.

Cal Newport. *So Good They Can't Ignore You: Why Skills Trump Passion in the Quest for Work You Love*. Business Plus, 2012.

Pasch, Ken. *Become the Boss You Always Wanted.* Descendants Press, 2010.

Peter, Laurence J. *The Peter Principle: Why Things Always Go Wrong.* Harper Business, Original 1969, updated 2009.

Peters, Tom. *In Search of Excellence.* G. K. Hall & Co, 1997.

Rath, Tom. *Strengths Finder 2.0.* Gallup Press, 2007.

Smith, Dean. *The Carolina Way.* Penguin Press, 2004.

Stanley, Thomas. *Stop Acting Rich and Start Living Like a Real Millionaire.* John Wiley & Sons, Inc., 2009.

Appendix E: Ideas to Improve the U.S. Political System

First, I believe we need to replace politicians with True Leaders. On balance, politicians are much more likely to believe in the Scarcity Mentality and assume an "I win" approach. A True Leader, scripted in the Abundance Mentality, would make decisions from a "We win" perspective. So why can't we interest more True Leaders in becoming involved in our governing bodies?

For years, I thought I had the job people fear most (public speaking!), but a recent Career Builder survey claimed that being a politician is the "scariest" job. Maybe that's what drives the Scarcity Mentality so prevalent among the group—another reason for fixing our system. If the rewards were more oriented toward a "We Win" perspective maybe that, in itself, would fix many issues. I've read reports about politicians who gain elective office as members of the middle class and a few years later make it into the ranks of the rich.

This should be disconcerting to us all. What have they "given" to reap those kinds of rewards?

Because of the importance of the decisions people in government make, I recommend we establish the following to help those True Leaders in governance positions remain true to their values. I offer them based on my expertise in human motivation. These implementations might also point to those who are not True Leaders.

1. Require that, before taking a position, leaders openly acknowledge and accept their responsibilities. The highest among these responsibilities would be to ensure their proposals provide the opportunity for each of us to Unlock, Engage, and Optimize our potential.

2. Have valid bases for measuring their performance.

3. Ensure that once they assume their respective positions, each of them is held accountable for not only the decisions they make but the outcomes of those decisions. This doesn't mean we erect a gallows on the courthouse lawn or form pitchfork gangs to enact justice. It does mean we hold these officials accountable for their decisions, especially those with OPM authority (management of Other People's Money).

4. In turn, we take seriously the right to support and vote for those we deem best qualified, and we stay engaged over time.

Here are further actions we might take:

Term Limits: Although most people who seek a governing position probably start out intending to make things better, natural outcomes take over once they assume a position of power. As historian and moralist John Emerich Edward Dalberg Acton—Lord Acton (1834–1902)—expressed in a letter to Bishop Mandell Creighton in 1887: "Power tends to corrupt, and absolute power corrupts absolutely. Great men are almost always bad men."

I don't believe all great people are bad people. However, people do have "tendencies" that must be addressed. Setting limits of how long a politician can be in office is a start.

Virtual Meetings: Why can't elected representatives live in their respective jurisdictions and be connected electronically to review, discuss/debate, and vote on matters of national importance? I'm concerned about the power culture that's formed in the nation's capital. Let's keep our representatives out of this culture and in the culture of the people they were elected to represent. (I realize this does nothing about the Executive branch, which is why I suggest only Phase 1 here. We have lots more work to do.)

Metrics Attached to All Bills: Politicians, like most people, don't like to be wrong— especially if it might hamper their efforts to be re-elected. To combat this problem, let's require legislators to build specific outcomes into each bill, including target completion dates. If these goals aren't achieved, the bill is automatically rescinded.

No Separate Perks Such as Retirement Packages: There should be no such thing as a retirement package for those who serve for short periods. Their goal shouldn't be to build their individual wealth but to enhance opportunities for all Americans. Compare the retirement package of those who risk their lives and suffer untold hardships defending our freedoms to the retirement package of those who serve one term in elected office at the federal level. I did, and what I found was appalling.

Five-Year Non-Compete: A contract could be required for all elected representatives and the crew members who work for those representatives: We need to ensure our legislators aren't setting themselves up for lucrative engagements once they've finished serving the people of this country. To that end, we could mandate they can't work for any organization or subsidiary of an organization that contracts with or receives funds from the government.

Zero-Based Budgeting: Those in business know how valuable this can be. If we require an annual re-justification of expenditures, it's likely we could drastically reduce fraud, waste, and abuse of our precious tax dollars.

Appendix F: Joe Tye, Values Coach, Inc., Bill of Responsibilities

(printed with permission)

The Bill of Responsibilities

The Authenticity Amendment
I will be true to myself, manage my ego and emotions so as to be civil and respectful to others, and shall not allow low self-esteem, self-limiting beliefs, or the negativity of others to prevent me from pursuing my authentic goals and dreams and becoming the unique individual I am meant to be.

The Integrity Amendment
Because integrity is the essential element of earned trust, I will tell the truth, keep my promises, live up to my commitments, and never violate my own integrity and the dignity of others by being judgmental or hypocritical.

The Awareness Amendment
Awareness being the essential element for personal happiness and professional success, as well as peace and harmony, I will pay attention to what is happening in the world around me, be empathetic to the needs and feelings of others, and monitor my emotional reactions to avoid becoming my own worst enemy.

The Courage Amendment
Because fear is a reaction and courage is a decision, I will make the commitment to stand up for what's right, stand up to those who do wrong, and do the things I know I need to despite my fears.

The Perseverance Amendment
Every great accomplishment having once been the seemingly "impossible" dream of a dreamer who refused to quit, I will accept the inevitability of obstacles and roadblocks with good cheer and equanimity, learn from my mistakes and failures, and never quit pursuing my authentic goals when the going gets tough.

The Faith Amendment
My faith in myself, in other people, and in the future will shine through in my attitudes and behaviors, and in open-hearted acceptance of those with beliefs that are different than mine.

The Purpose Amendment
I will commit to a purpose bigger than "what's in it for me" goals and define an overarching purpose to give meaning to my work and life.

The Vision Amendment
I will contribute to creating a common shared vision for a better world, and commit to action that will help to transform the good intentions of today into the reality of tomorrow.

The Focus Amendment
I will be a good steward in how I spend my time, energy, and financial resources in order to concentrate on achieving the goals and dreams that really matter, and that help to make the world a better place for current and future generations.

The Enthusiasm Amendment
I will approach my days with a positive attitude, seek to discern the best in every other person and situation, do my work with a spirit of mission, and seek to restore the passion of youth with curiosity, humor, and a smile.

The Service Amendment
I will help others in need, be generous in spirit and means, and take time to replenish my own spirit so that I may continue to serve others.

The Leadership Amendment
Because we all have the opportunity to be leaders, I will, through my example, set high expectations for myself and others, and seek to inspire and influence others to always do what is best for the common good.

The Bill of Responsibilities is adapted from the Values Coach Inc. course on *The Twelve Core Action Values*™.

Values Coach Inc., Jordan Creek Plaza, PO Box 490, Solon, IA, 52333

ENDNOTES

[1] Maslow's Hierarchy of Needs: https://en.wikipedia.org/wiki/Maslow%27s_hierarchy_of_needs

[2] https://newworkplace.wordpress.com/2013/09/05/does-the-dunning-kruger-effect-help-to-explain-bad-bosses-and-overrated-co-workers/

[3] Attribution Theory; http://www.leadership-central.com/attribution-theory.html#axzz4GCeDXgKp

[4] Excerpt from Chamberlain "Peace in Our Time" speech at the Heston Aerodrome near London, UK on September 30, 1938. http://www.emersonkent.com/speeches/peace_in_our_time.htm

[5] Excerpt from Churchill's "Blood, Toil, Sweat, and Tears" speech in the British House of Commons on May 13, 1940. http://www.emersonkent.com/speeches/blood_toil_tears_and_sweat.htm

[6] Excerpt from Hitler's "The Jewish Question" speech at Berlin, Germany on January 30, 1939. http://www.emersonkent.com/speeches/the_jewish_question.htm

[7]   Habits 1, 2, & 3. Dr. Stephen R. Covey, *7 Habits of Highly Effective People,* Free Press, 1990.

[8]   "What Do Millennials Want From Your Workplace?" https://smallbiztrends.com/2016/08/what-do-millennials-want-at-work.html

[9]   "Hoosiers connection to reality" http://www.chasingthefrog.com/reelfaces/hoosiers.php

[10]   http://www.johnmaxwell.com/blog/do-you-have-what-it-takes

[11]   https://en.wikiquote.org/wiki/Helmuth_von_Moltke_the_Elder

[12]   http://www.brainyquote.com/quotes/quotes/d/dwight-dei164720.html

[13]   Dave Matheny, "Overeager," *Sport Aviation,* August 2015.

[14]   http://www.todayifoundout.com/index.php/2011/11/post-it-notes-were-invented-by-accident/

[15]   Pennsylvania's Film Production Tax Credit and Industry Analysis; http://filminpa.com/wp-content/uploads/2009/07/PaFilm-ProductionIndustryAnalysis.pdf

[16]   Andrew S. Grove, *High Output Management,* Vintage; 2nd edition, 1995. p. 111.

[17]   Wikipedia: "Black swan" is a metaphor that describes a surprise event that has a major effect and is often inappropriately rationalized after the fact with the benefit of hindsight; https://en.wikipedia.org/wiki/Black_swan_theory

[18]   Wikpedia: Zero-based budgeting is a method of budgeting in which all expenses start from a "zero base" and must be justified for each new period. Every function within an organization is analyzed for its needs and costs. https://en.wikipedia.org/wiki/Zero-based_budgeting

[19] Wikipedia: History of Japan: although it would take multiple inclusions to understand the entire story, this entry provides a glimpse: https://en.wikipedia.org/wiki/History_of_Japan

[20] "Ben Bernanke Was Incredibly, Uncannily Wrong" https://mises.org/library/ben-bernanke-was-incredibly-uncannily-wrong

[21] https://www.youtube.com/watch?v=9n5shmX_eiM

[22] https://www.youtube.com/watch?v=MDD4IkVZWTM

[23] The Smart Career Move You Haven't Considered: Working Abroad; http://www.forbes.com/sites/dailymuse/2013/10/11/the-smart-career-move-you-havent-considered-working-abroad/#2c26669e38ad

[24] Wikipedia: Yuri Gagarin https://en.wikipedia.org/wiki/Yuri_Gagarin

[25] NASA Technologies Benefit Our Lives; https://spinoff.nasa.gov/Spinoff2008/tech_benefits.html

[26] Creative Destruction; http://www.econlib.org/library/Enc/CreativeDestruction.html

[27] https://www.amazon.com/s/ref=nb_sb_noss_2?url=-search-alias%3Daps&field-keywords=Tao+Te+Ching+-by+Lao+Tzu

[28] Jim Collins and Jerry I. Porras, *Built to Last: Successful Habits of Visionary Companies,* Harper Business Essentials, 2004.

[29] "Progress Cleaning the Air and Improving People's Health."https://www.epa.gov/clean-air-act-overview/progress-cleaning-air-and-improving-peoples-health

[30] "U.S. education spending tops global list, study shows" http://www.cbsnews.com/news/us-education-spending-tops-global-list-study-shows/ "American Schools vs. the World: Expensive,

Unequal, Bad at Math" http://www.theatlantic.com/education/archive/2013/12/american-schools-vs-the-world-expensive-unequal-bad-at-math/281983/

[31] "The Impact of Federal Involvement in America's Classrooms" http://www.cato.org/publications/congressional-testimony/impact-federal-involvement-americas-classrooms

[32] http://nypost.com/2016/04/11/demand-is-overwhelming-to-get-kids-into-charter-schools/

[33] "All Students Are Created Equally (and Differently)" https://teach.com/what/teachers-teach/learning-styles/

[34] "Sonya Carson's devotion to her sons' development" http://www.historyswomen.com/amazingmoms/SonyaCarson.html

[35] "Around 1,700 private jets flying in to Davos" http://www.dailymail.co.uk/travel/travel_news/article-2916539/World-Economic-Forum-Skies-Switzerland-double-number-private-jets.html

[36] "Electronic Doomsday for the US?" https://www.gatestoneinstitute.org/7214/electro-magnetic-pulse-emp

[37] Joe Tye Bill of Responsibilities; https://www.facebook.com/joetyevaluescoach/posts/1043667069005475

Morgan James
Speakers Group

www.TheMorganJamesSpeakersGroup.com

We connect Morgan James published authors with live and online events and audiences whom will benefit from their expertise.

Printed in the USA
CPSIA information can be obtained
at www.ICGtesting.com
JSHW022321140824
68134JS00019B/1223

9 781683 505136